Around Historic Sussex

with Ray Miller

Drawings by Gerald Lip

MIDAS BOOKS

Shoreham Lighthouse

For the past ten years Ray Miller and Gerald Lip have combed Sussex for facts of antiquity and interest that lie hidden behind the architecture of the past and their articles and illustrations over this period have been seen by the many readers of the Brighton Evening Argus. In this beautifully illustrated book there are some 144 examples of their historical investigation, from Bognor in the West, Rye in the East and Crawley in the North. Churches, pubs, castles, abbeys, windmills, lighthouses, martello towers, market towns, famous houses, seaside towns, village streets, shopping areas vividly portray the character that makes Sussex such a distinctive county.

Ray Miller is a journalist on the Brighton Evening Argus and lives in Brighton. He is married with two children.

Gerald Lip is an illustrator on the Daily Express, is married, and lives in Hove.

m

First published 1976 by:
MIDAS BOOKS
12 Dene Way, Speldhurst,
Tunbridge Wells, Kent. TN3 ONX.

Front cover design by David Morley-Clarke.

ISBN 0 85936 071 7

Printed in Great Britain by Chapel River Press, Andover, Hampshire.
Produced by Time Brokers.

Heathfield

FOREWORD

Sussex is a beautiful county and nothing pleases me more than to live here. Despite being near to London it still has all the values I look for in countryside — greenery, beautiful gardens and a rich history.

It is in that particular connection I find these articles such a useful guide. History is one of those things you can sense but sometimes it's a hunt to find historic details that complete the picture. Here in this book there's a wealth of them and I hope they will make your journey round Sussex one of adventure and continual interest.

Yours
Vera Lynn

Dame Vera Lynn

Contents and Illustrations

Lewes

North End House, Rottingdean 1
Shoreham Lighthouse 2
Gibraltar Tower, Heathfield 3
Foreword, Dame Vera Lynn 3
Alciston 7
Alfriston, Drusillas 8
Alfriston, Clergy House 9
Arundel, The Black Rabbit 10
Arundel, The Castle 11
Arundel, The Cathedral 12
Balcombe 13
Barcombe, The Mill 14
Battle, The Abbey 15
Battle, Pilgrim's Rest 16
Bayham, The Abbey 17
Beeding, Lower, Leonardslee 18
Beeding, Upper, Smith's Folly 19
Beeding, Lower, South Lodge 20
Bexhill, Old Town 21
Bexhill, Manor House 22
Billingshurst 23
Birling Gap, Bardolph Hall 24
Bishopstone , The Manor 25
Bognor, Hotham Park House 26
Bognor 27
Bolney 28
Bolney, The Lodge 29
Bosham 30
Bramber, House of Pipes 31
Bramber 32
Brighton, The Lanes 33
Brighton, Royal Pavilion 34
Brighton, Lewes Crescent 35
Brighton, Mount Sion Place 36
Brighton, Roedean School 37
Brighton, Hangleton Manor 38
Brighton, Clock Tower 39
Brighton, St. Peter's Church 40
Brighton, Royal Pavilion North Gate 41
Brighton, The College 42
Brighton, The Dome 43
Burpham 44
Burwash 45
Bury 46
Chailey 47
Chelwood Gate, Birch Grove House 48
Chelwood Gate, Chelworth House 49

Henfield, Woods Mill

Chelwood Gate 50
Chichester 51
Chichester, Market Cross 52
Chichester, Old Cross Hotel 53
Chilgrove, White Horse Inn 54
Clayton, St. John the Baptist Church 55
Cocking, The Mill House 56
Cowfold, Brook Farm House 57
Cowfold, St. Hugh's Charterhouse Monastery 58
Crawley, Ancient House Restaurant 59
Cuckfield 60
Cuckfield, The Park 61
Ditchling 62
Eastbourne, Old Town 63
Eastbourne, Prince Albert 64
East Dean, Lavant Valley 65
East Dean, Nr. Eastbourne 66
East Grinstead 67
East Grinstead, Sackville College 68
Etchingham Church 69
Falmer 70
Felpham 71
Findon 72
Fishbourne 73
Fittleworth, Mill House 74
Fletching 75
Forest Row 76
Fulking, Shepherd and Dog 77
Fulking 78
Glyndebourne, Glynde Place 79
Handcross, Nymans 80
Hardham Priory 81
Hastings, Fishermen's Church 82
Hastings, Dickens Cottage 83
Hastings, Pulpit Gate 84
Haywards Heath, Heaselands House 85
Haywards Heath, Borde Hill House 86
Henfield 87
Herstmonceux Castle 88
Hickstead 89
High Salvington, The Windmill 90
Hooe, The Lamb Inn 91
Houghton Bridge 92
Hurstpierpoint 93
Kingston, Shoreham Grammar School 94
Lancing, The School and Chapel 95
Lewes, The Castle 96

Pevensey Castle

Lindfield, Old Place 97
Lindfield 98
Littlington 99
Lullington Church 100
Midhurst, Cowdray House 101
Midhurst 102
Midhurst, Cowdray Castle 103
Newhaven 104
Ovingdean 105
Peacehaven 106
Pett 107
Petworth, Lombard Street 108
Pevensey 109
Piddinghoe 110
Polegate Windmill 111
Poling, St. John's Priory 112
Poynings 113
Rodmell, Monk's House 114
Rottingdean, Tallboys 115
Rusper, Old Cottages 116
Rye, Gibbet Mill 117
Rye, Mermaid Street 118
St. Leonards, Clock House 119
Seaford, Martello Tower 120
Shipley Windmill 121
Slindon 122
Slindon, Dedisham Manor 123
Slindon College 124
Stopham 125
Small Dole, The Golding Barn 126
Sompting Church 127
Sheffield Park 128
Shoreham 129
Southease Church 130
Southwick 131
Steyning 132
Steyning, Chanctonbury Cottage 133
Storrington, Parham House 134
Thakeham 135
Trotton, Terwick Mill 136
Warnham, Field Place 137
West Burton, Cooke's House 138
Westdean, Charleston Manor 139
Westham 140
Winchelsea, The Armoury 141
Winchelsea Church 142
Withyham, Dorset Arms 143
Worthing 144

Alciston

Monks in bygone centuries must have spoken the name of Alciston in more than their usual tones of reverence. Then, as now, it was a secluded hamlet of a few houses nestling in the countryside below Firle Beacon east of Lewes.

But in those days it had the distinction of being what many a hard pressed cleric would find useful today — a kind of religious holiday camp.

The small church at Alciston was once a dependency of Battle Abbey, and it was to the more cloistered calm of countryside and nature that monks came for a rest from the rigours and discipline of monastic life.

Alciston has lost nothing in restfulness over the years. Court House Farm, close to the small round churchyard, is a medieval building with many ancient walls providing tangible proof of the ecclesiastical establishment that once flourished here.

More recent history sleuths in the hamlet have also discovered a 14th century dovecote which had almost given up the battle with age and ivy but which has now been restored.

But if it's just a plain glimpse of beautiful country you're seeking, try the view across the village pond through the trees and along the Downs to Lewes.

Alfriston

The zoo inhabitants of Drusilla's owe their present home to the founder, Capt. Louis Douglas Ann. He it was who with his wife came here in 1923.

The centre of the farm he took over was the cottage that had been used by generations who had tilled the fertile soils of this corner of Alfriston. But to many visitors it is the charming 16th century barn and its newly thatched roof that also symbolises the old world atmosphere of Drusilla's.

Once cattle used to shelter here from the worst of winter. Today it is a restaurant, tea-room and ballroom where thousands of visitors pass through yearly.

It's a far cry today from the times where the farm had become derelict and when a bone mill was set up to produce farm fertiliser.

The emphasis now is on helping people appreciate live animals rather than making use of dead ones. There are now different breeds of cattle and Drusilla's works in conjunction with the Rare Breeds Survival Trust to make people aware that there are more than just Jerseys and Herefords in the cattle world.

They rent 107 acres of the new Seven Sisters Country Park from East Sussex County Council as pastures for the herd.

Alfriston

Looked at from any direction, the Clergy House at Alfriston is historic. It's one of the few remaining pre-Reformation clergy houses left — an example of genuine domestic architecture dating from around 1350.

In 1896 it became the first building acquired by the National Trust. The cost. Just £10!

In the 17th century a parish register mentions it as the home of the parish priest. Later, with the clergy wanting higher living standards, the old house gradually fell into disrepair.

It was used for a time as a labourer's cottage and seemed destined to become a ruin before the fledgling National Trust came to the rescue.

In 1890 the Ecclesiastical Commissioners appeared to have little interest in preserving ancient buildings.

They proposed to demolish the property and probably would have done so if the vicar and the Sussex Archaeological Society had not protested.

The preservationist zeal enables visitors today to study the oak framing construction of the house.

The space between the stout oak supports is filled with traditional wattle and daub and the central hall, with its tie-beams and king-posts, once served as a communal living room.

It's this original medieval room that is open to the public for most of the year. The remainder of the property can be viewed on appointment only.

Arundel

The Black Rabbit pub is by the River Arun with stirring views of Arundel Castle and the whole picturesque sweep of the Sussex countryside.

Apart from its title — and no one knows the derivation — the Black Rabbit has more than a few other unusual features in its colourful past.

The Black Rabbit was probably built as accommodation for bargees and it doubtless benefitted in 1861 with the opening of a waterway between the Arun and the River Wey and London.

Eventually the railways killed off that part of the pub's history when the canal became derelict in the late 1800's.

But the first known licensee had seen his time behind the bars there by then. He was one John Olliver, who is recorded as the first Rabbit publican in 1804 — a family link which was to stretch onwards for another 70 years.

Further insight on their reign may come to light with the discovery recently of an ancient diary. It goes back to at least 1894 and recently helped manager David Smith assist a lady with a more than unusual request — namely when and in what room did one of her relatives stop at the Black Rabbit in 1894.

But the demise of canals didn't see the end of the pub. Arundel was by then beginning to attract more of a residential population, as were towns along the South Coast.

It was they who took the bargees' places at the bars and eventually in the restaurant that was formed from the old stables.

Arundel

The seat of the Duke of Norfolk, Arundel Castle, or rather its site, dates back to the Norman conquest when Roger de Montgomery built a castle before 1086 on land previously occupied by a Saxon fortress.

Apart from the odd siege, all was well for some centuries until Oliver Cromwell. In 1642 Arundel fell to the parliamentary forces while the earl was away.

He recaptured it only to have it taken again in 1643 by Sir William Waller and to suffer further the ignominy of having the place demolished around 1651.

Luckily for Arundel, the Dukes of Norfolk had more staying power than Oliver. The 8th Duke busied himself restoring the seat in 1720.

Then there's the lofty church of St. Philip Neri, now Roman Catholic cathedral for Arundel and Brighton.

The cathedral was built from 1869-73 for the 15th Duke of Norfolk in the French Gothic style.

If you've energy left after walking round these two palaces of stone try a walk down the High Street, bounded on one side by the castle wall. Here you'll find the Norfolk Arms, a brick-fronted coaching house; opposite, a grocer's shop with a moulded plaster ceiling with the crest of Fitzalans and, higher up, some beautiful Georgian terraces.

In Tarrant Street George Macdonald, the Scottish novelist and poet, was appointed pastor of the Congregational Church.

And in Maltravers Street is the castellated town hall, dating back to the 1830's.

Arundel

It was in 1965 the first announcement was made that the church of St. Philip of Neri was to be made into Arundel Cathedral to head the newly formed diocese of Arundel and Brighton.

It is this splendid hilltop church that has provided a new religious focal point and identity for Roman Catholics throughout Sussex and parts of Surrey.

Arundel Cathedral was founded by the 15th Duke of Norfolk. He commissioned the building on his coming of age in 1868 and it was opened to its first worshippers on July 1, 1873.

The architects employed became a household word, but not for designing buildings. They were the firm of Joseph Aloysius Hansom, famous as the designers of Victorian edifices, Birmingham Town Hall — but most famous for the Hansom cab that was the invention of Mr. Hansom himself.

The 15th Duke of Norfolk was a great admirer of Gothic architecture. He and the cathedral's builders could think of no more superior position for the building than the top of Parson's Hill opposite the walls of Arundel Castle and the landmark for miles around.

But the site was far from perfect in other respects. To support the 280ft. spire foundations had to be sunk more than 50ft. into the hillside. Even with that precaution by the Victorian builders emergency work was carried out only a few years ago to prevent further sinking of the cathedral's marble floor.

Yet built it was and it was soon noted for the geometrically shaped windows — especially the splendid wheel window at the west end.

Balcombe

Balcombe lies 17 miles north of Brighton, 4 from Cuckfield and is 33 miles from London. That places it fair and square in one of the greenest, quietest parts of East Sussex.

The landscape is of gentle wooded hills and tranquil streams flowing down to the Ouse. In a valley to the east is a beautiful lake, a former hammer pond much frequented by freshwater fishermen.

Further downstream, on the Shill Brook, is the charming mill house for which the Balcombe area is so well known.

The village itself exudes an air of weathered maturity. The church of St. Mary is constructed in stone and has mixed architectural styles.

The register dates from 1539 and the list of rectors goes back to 1333.

The church itself has a 15th century tower with a spire containing a clock and eight bells — two were added to celebrate the jubilee of King George V.

There are nine stained glass windows and the church's interior was restored in 1851 and again in 1873.

In the area too are health springs and quarries that used to provide stone for the parish and neighbourhood. Once something of more immediate worth was found.

On May 24, 1897, a metal pot holding 12 gold and 742 silver coins was uncovered in the village. But that was quickly claimed by the Crown as treasure trove.

But such things are only of transient value. The restful qualities of countryside that make up Balcombe cannot be taken away so easily.

Barcombe

It's hardly surprising that Barcombe Mills is a centre for two of the most pastoral pursuits the countryside has to offer — painting and fishing.

There is hardly a place in Sussex that offers such a blending of river and countryside and in such a beautiful setting of watercolour tranquility.

Barcombe is mentioned in the Domesday Book as Bircham. More than that, it is recorded as having had three and a half mills at the time.

The three mills were straightforward enough. Where the anomaly is believed to have crept in is with a mill house built over the river.

The water wheel was reputed to have been exactly in the middle of the stream. So because half of the mill house was on one and the other resting on the opposite bank in the parish of Isfield the Domesday chroniclers decided that Barcombe was only entitled to half a share in the historic inventory.

These days the mills of Barcombe are just a memory as the Ouse flows gently by. In the later times of milling here there was a windmill, a flour mill and an oil mill for making oilcake for cattle. In those prosperous days a branch line of the London, Brighton and South Coast Railway used to run up to the edge of the river and along to the bank to take away the produce of Sussex farming.

The river itself was easily navigable then and barges, too, made the journey to Barcombe.

There is more to the district, of course, than just the mills area. The village of Barcombe Cross is a mile and a half away, near where the Roman road from London to Lewes crossed the Ouse and the Sussex Greensand Way.

Battle

Historically there is no more singularly significant place in Sussex or England than Battle.

The books and the stories have chronicled it all, how Harold raced south after his victory over the Northern invaders at Stamford Bridge, how William the eventual conqueror landed at Pevensey on September 28 and eventually how the Normans finally triumphed over English courage with shrewd French stratagem.

It was a point which marked the beginning of a new nation — and the new town of Battle. It grew up around the abbey founded by William the Conqueror in thanksgiving for his victory.

Battle today is virtually a high street on a hill, where visitors gaze at the old pharmacy of 1500 vintage, at the old almonry, of 15th and 17th century origin and higher up the picturesque old houses of Market Place.

But it is the Abbey itself, with its massive 14th century gatehouse which enshrines the memories for which the town is famous throughout the world.

Originally the Abbey was settled by Benedictine monks from Marmoutier in northern France and the completed church was dedicated to St. Martin of Tours in 1094 by St. Anselm, the Archbishop of Canterbury. It was a ceremony performed before William Rufus himself and the greatest barons and most important clergy of the day.

He obviously had something worth defending for at its dissolution in 1583 The Abbey was one of the richest in the land. But that soon changed. It was handed over to Sir Anthony Browne, Master of the King's Horse to Henry VIII and later the church and cloisters were pulled down and the abbot's lodgings converted into a dwelling house.

It was in 1857 that they were finally restored to house today the famous girl's school.

Battle

The Pilgrim's Rest at Battle dates back to about 1420 and sits today at a slightly lower level than a pleasantly laid out front garden.

In the accounts of the bedell, or bailiff, of Battle Abbey of 1420-21, he is granted "an allowance of 2s. 4d. for the gate next the almonry because in the hands of the almoner for two years."

In other words, this was a remission of rent for rebuilding the Priest's House.

Still owned today by the abbey estate, this building's prime purpose was as a House of God where impoverished wayfarers and travellers could stay for a night.

It isn't certain that they were always pilgrims. That word was used in a more general sense, for there were no saints' shrines at the abbey and Battle wasn't on any direct pilgrim route.

But what the house certainly did was offer a night's accommodation for poor travellers, many of whom were doubtless on their way to the coast to sail overseas from Hastings.

If those same travellers passed through Battle today they would still recognise the resting place of their overnight stop.

It is the only house in the High Street to have escaped Georgian re-fronting and to have retained its timber work exposed in all the original freshness.

Bayham

Bayham Abbey, on the Sussex-Kent border, just north of Wadhurst, has been described as the most impressive monastic ruin in Sussex. The lavish description must stretch also to the location that was chosen by the Premonstratensian canons when they came from Premontre, in France, in 1208.

Bayham has what the Department of the Environment describes as the most complete monastic ruins in Lowland England. Part of that tribute is thanks to the durable Sussex sandstone which the canons used for their abbey. The site was given to them by a crusader, Robert de Turnham.

But the Premonstratensians had slightly different ideas about what devotion demanded as compared with the Cistercians. Their ideals and their abbey were simple and austere yet when it came to day-to-day living the routine was less spartan.

Bayham represented an amalgamation of two abbeys which had been built on sites the canons subsequently weren't too keen on — Brockley in Kent and Otham in Sussex. They named as their chief patrons the Sackvilles of Buckhurst and among their early visitors was St. Richard the Bishop of Chichester.

As part of the power politics of the Middle Ages the abbey was prematurely closed down by Wolsey in 1525.

What the public sees now when they go to Bayham is a splendid collection of buildings ranging from the gatehouse, which was converted into a lakeside summerhouse in the 18th century, to the 15th century church which constitutes the north range and leads to the cloister and eventually to the obscured west range, which contained the abbot's guesthall and on its upper floor his chambers.

The original east range remains and is made up of a sacristy, the chapter house vestibule, with a taller chapter house projecting from it.

Beeding

Sir Edmund Loder himself laid the foundations of what has become the flower of Sussex gardens — Leonardslee.

The first steps towards laying out grounds that have now achieved national fame among gardeners were taken by Sir Edmund in 1887.

He had at his disposal one of the most magnificent sites in the Home Counties. The family house — still occupied by the Loder family — was built by them in 1855 and stands 300ft. above sea level looking down on the rolling South Downs.

The gardens themselves are situated in the village of Lower Beeding (on the main Brighton to Horsham road) and are at the southern end of the ancient forest of St. Leonard. At the bottom of the terrace, in front of the house, is a small stream which grows into a series of lakes. They are more than just an extra setting to the natural beauty.

Once they were hammer ponds used for the flourishing Sussex iron-ore industry, when dams were built across them and the water power harnessed to work furnace bellows and wheel hammers which fashioned the crude metal.

The background to the gardens is one of weather-worn old oak, beech and birch intermingled with conifers. And the soil from which such a proliferation of plants and trees spring is a light loam.

The final combination which makes for perfection at Leonardslee is its valley sheltering against strong winds from north and east, and an average rainfall of 28in. to provide a balanced ration of water.

When Sir Edmund began his work he did at least have a start. Some of the large Californian redwoods and Wellingtonias were already stretching into the heavens. But his particular love was for rhododendrons and camellias and today the massed banks of blooms attract thousands of visitors when the gardens are open for their six spring weeks from April until June.

Beeding

It looks like a hybrid product of Bavaria and the Loire, all turrets, chateau spirals and medieval-type windows you'd expect a fairytale princess to be wooed from.

Except that the building happens to be in Upper Beeding and the girls you'll see are pupils of the Convent of the Blessed Sacrament.

They've come a long way from Smith's Folly. According to local knowledge that is what the remarkable Sussex building used to be known as.

Smith was a Victorian gentleman reputed to have commissioned it something over 100 years ago and then to have gone bankrupt before it was finished.

Hunting appears to have been its purpose but whether Mr. Smith ever sallied forth from this extravagant lodge to anything other than a line-up of creditors is not known.

What is for sure is that the nuns moved in during the year 1903 so that the school last year was able to celebrate its 70th birthday.

The early years of the century saw many religious schools driven out and forbidden to teach in France and it was on October 10 in 1903 that five pupils and two sisters left Paris for Beeding.

After they had travelled wearily through a village lit only by their lanterns the children arrived at a most unschool-like place. There were tapestries on the walls, heads of deer on the great staircase walls and a hall filled with exotic plants.

Over the years the nuns have brought about many improvements and extensions to the school.

The school was recognised by the Department of Education and Science in 1957.

Beeding

You have to be a stickler for names to harp on the distinction between Upper and Lower Beeding. To people who have a feeling for the countryside the unifying factor is that both villages are prime examples of Sussex at its green and verdant best. Just for the record the name difference is probably a geographical one and not a mark of class distinction.

The one Beeding is higher above sea level than the other. At one time both had close links, despite Lower Beeding being ten miles to the north and nearer Horsham than its sister village. But the two were made separate parishes in 1830.

Originally it is likely that the Saxon name for the area was Beding and in the Domesday Book there is a reference to Beddinges. Roman remains were unearthed 150 years ago. It was the perfect place for Victorian farmer and scientist Mr. F.D. Godman. He built South Lodge in 1883 at Lower Beeding, a house at the entrance to St. Leonard's Forest.

The building itself is a splendid example of mock Jacobean architecture and stands on the site of a former house. Mr. Godman was an eminent ornithologist, sportsman and natural scientist. One of his greatest achievements was a 40 volume natural history of Central America. He was also the keenest of horticulturalists. When he built South Lodge there was no garden, now there are extensive gardens opened to the public on Sunday afternoons.

Bexhill

History takes Bexhill back to 772, to the times of King Offa of Mercia. He granted land at Bixlea—meaning box wood—for the endowment of a church under the jurisdiction of the Bishop of Selsey. But with the arrival of the Norman conquest Bexhill was presented as a manor to Robert, Count of Eu, who built Hastings Castle.

In 1148 it was given back to the bishops of Chichester, who succeeded those of Selsey, and they promptly consolidated their position by building themselves a fortified manor house.

Years later, under Henry VIII, the manor was taken by the Crown, but during the reign of Elizabeth I it came into the hands of Lord Buckhurst, whose descendants were the earls of Dorset and De La Warr and who have retained their family link ever since. The earls were materially responsible for promoting the growth of Bexhill to its size today. But in 1881 it had a population of little more than 2,000 and it was only in the late 1800's that its expansion-proper began.

The parish church reflected the development with a considerable rebuilding about the same time, although its history dates back to about 1070. On an inside wall is a carved stone, possibly from the grave of a Saxon child or perhaps the cover of a reliquary that at one time could have held the remains of an outstanding religious personage.

Bexhill

It was in AD 772 that King Offa II of Mercia made the grant of a charter to found and endow a church in a quiet coastal corner of Sussex.

The building was to become known as St. Peter's and the town that grew up around it is Bexhill.

The paradox is that Bexhill today is almost entirely new yet possesses a past stretching right back to Saxon times.

In 477 a band of Saxon adventurers under their chieftain Aella established themselves on the low-lying headland of Selsey Bill. They captured Regnum, now known as Chichester, and in 490 overran the Roman-British fortress of Anderida at Pevensey Castle.

Before the Norman Conquest the manor of Bexhill was vested in the See of Selsey, but was laid waste by the Normans after the 1066 invasion. Norman's Bay, where William the Conqueror "kissed the sand" is within the modern borough of Bexhill though the once great haven where they came ashore has long silted up to form part of Pevensey Level.

The manor was later granted to a prominent Norman, the Count of Eu, and Bexhill went on to be mentioned in the Domesday Book.

It wasn't until 1148 that it was restored to the See of Chichester and the Manor House was probably rebuilt by Sir Richard de la Wycke, Bishop of Chichester, around 1250.

Under the Tudor devastation of the great religious houses, the Manor of Bexhill passed to the Crown but in the reign of Elizabeth I, Lord Buckhurst was "seized of the manor" and through him it passed to the Dorset family and the ninth Earl De La Warr. Today the remains are owned by Bexhill Corporation.

Billingshurst

It was the Romans who helped put Billingshurst on the map. Or more specifically an engineer called Belinus.

Back in the days of their occupation, Chichester early developed as an important regional centre. The need consequently arose for good communications with legions based in London.

So Belinus ordered a direct link between the two cities to be built. It's undeviating route became known as Stane Street—the longest street in the county and one that runs right through the middle of Billingshurst along the route of the modern A29 main London to Bognor road.

Billingshurst is thought to have come by its name from an old Saxon family once prominent in the area.

They were known as the Billings and they also lent their name to Billingsgate, London's fish market.

Today Billingshurst represents the first real village-cum-town once you've passed the spreading urban development of Horsham and Crawley.

Yet it was once a vastly poorer area. The town had its definite beginnings in the reign of Edward the Confessor. He helped bring people here by giving huge tracts of land in the neighbourhood to the French Abbey of Fecamp, in Normandy.

They used the acres for timber, and later for crops, cattle and the collecting of acorns for pigs. With cultivation came more people to settle, notably blacksmiths and later iron smelters who set up many hammer ponds in this Sussex corner.

In Henry the Third's reign Billingshurst suffered three plagues.

Unchanged above it all stands the Church of St. Mary, with its elegant spire rising high above the Weald.

Birling Gap

It was the Beorls who gave Birling Gap its name. They were a war-like tribe of Saxon sea rovers who harassed the coast of Sussex before settling outside of what is modern Eastbourne in 489.

They chose the only break in the white towering cliffs between Holywell and Cuckmere Haven, a distance of nearly seven miles.

And they made way for William the Conqueror, his half brother Robert, Earl of Mortain, who eventually came into possession of the manor, and later the building in the middle of the 1200s of Bardolph Hall.

After the Norman invasion, Birling passed from the Earl of Mortain, via the Lords of Pevensey, to Hugh de Gurnay. But his successor fell out with the ruling authorities and the manor passed over in forfeit to the de Cressek family.

It wasn't until 1225 that it was restored to the Gurnays and Juliana, the last of the line, married William Bardolph.

They were the builders of Bardolph Hall, a building in which the family lived from its construction around 1250 and which still stands to this day as a reminder of early South Coast forerunners.

The Bardolph family stayed there for two hundred peaceful years until they lost Birling after the Wars of the Roses, when the Queen was lady of the manor for a short period.

The year 1565 saw Birling held by Frances Carew, later Sir Christopher Carew, whose family probably went on to build the manor house. And from then, down to more modern times, a succession of people lived at Bardolph Hall.

Bishopstone

Centuries ago the bishops of Chichester had an eye enough for beautiful countryside to build themselves a manor called Bishopstone in a secluded and fertile valley barely two miles from Seaford.

And today it still has a link with those religious days in the shape of one of the loveliest churches in Sussex.

Its most notable feature is simply its age. Hardly a part of the building is dated later than early 13th century.

The nave walls and the large south porch date back directly to the Saxons and are of 9th or 10th century vintage. The Normans too left their mark. The tower chancel and north aisle are all Norman work of the 12th century.

Above a gabled doorway is a Saxon sun-dial carved with the name of Eadric and built into the south wall of the Norman tower is a highly unusual coffin-slab of the 12th century showing a lamb and doves drinking, all entwined in a cable.

Bishopstone is the place you'd expect to inspire poetry and in the church is a wall memorial tablet to the Rev. James Hurdis, who was vicar of the parish almost until his death in 1801 and who in his day was renowned as a Sussex poet.

As a hamlet of peace and seclusion on the ever busy Coast, Bishopstone today is an unwritten ode to the charm of Sussex.

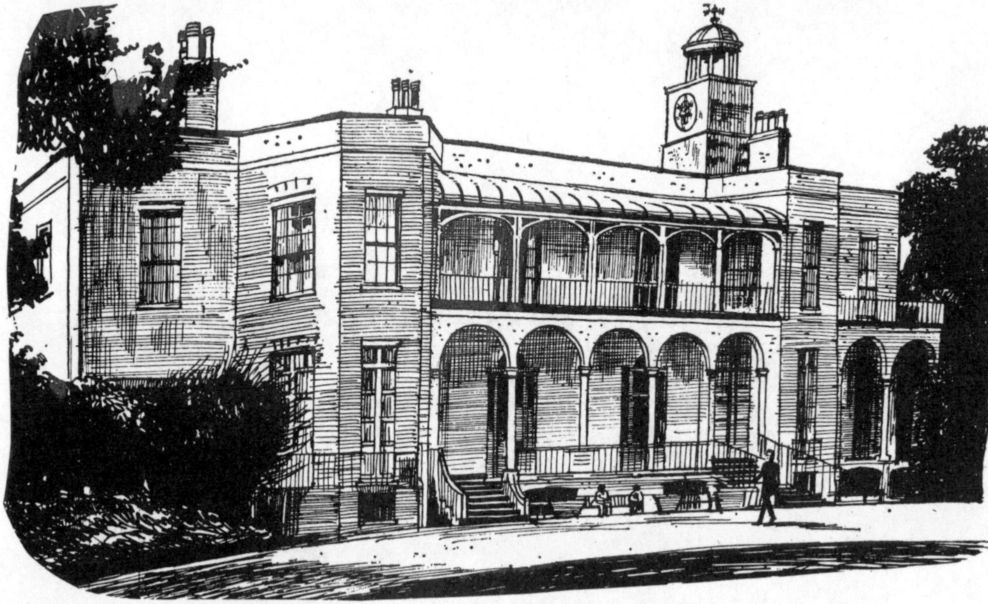

Bognor

Hotham Park House was built in 1792 by Sir Richard Hotham, Bognor's founder. Sir Richard was a Southwark hatter who brought his money to these parts of the South Coast in the 1780's and settled in Bersted, a mile inland.

There he built an assembly hall and hotel and labelled the whole project Hothampton. It wasn't entirely successful because Bognor sprang up on the coastline and proved itself the bigger attraction. But Sir Richard wasn't deterred. He had built for himself the Hotham private residence that is today's preservationist tussle.

Early last century it was renamed Bersted Lodge and then again it was later redubbed Aldwick Manor. At this time it was occupied by one Mr. W.H.F. Fletcher, who was the Lord of the Manor of Aldwick.

The house stayed with the Fletchers until 1941 and was purchased by Bognor council in 1946, together with 75 acres of woods and greens, for the trifling sum of £40,000.

Things at that stage looked all set for a bright future. The Hotham estate was opened to the public in 1947 and about the same period the house itself was leased to the Ministry of Works as a national insurance office. But Bognor itself had no insurance against the ravages of time.

When the civil servants moved out civil engineers moved in and immediately said the building needed a steel inner girdle to hold it together. That was the beginning of the all-too-familiar spiral of rising preservationist costs, desperate efforts by the Friends of Hotham Park House and finally a demolition request by the local council.

At one time it was hoped to house the Guermonprez Collection here — all £60,000 worth of birds in flight, Sussex flora and fauna, 120,000 seashells, 150 big game heads and more.

It was left to the townspeople of Bognor but after dampness gnawed its way through to some of the exhibits the exhibition had to be disbanded and sent to Portsmouth while Hotham Park House hung derelict in the balance.

Bognor

The name Bognor betrays a Saxon origin. In the Middle Ages Bognor was a fishing hamlet. But it wasn't until the end of the 18th century that a Southwark hatter, Sir Richard Hotham, started the train of residential events that led to the extensive coastal town that exists today.

Bognor is sheltered on the north by the South Downs and is about halfway between Selsey Bill and the mouth of the Arun at Littlehampton. And unlike less fortunate resorts elsewhere in Sussex it boasts beaches with a fair share of sand.

This, together with its fair share of sunshine throughout the year, attracted George V here after his serious illness in 1928. So Bognor became Rognor Regis.

Sir Richard might have seen it as the fulfilment of a dream. He had spent some £60,000 trying to attract the nobility of George III's time here. At one time he even tried to change the town's name to Hothampton to give it a new image.

Indeed it was to encourage a visit from the royalty of the day that Sir Richard was rumoured to have built the manor house in Hotham Park that still bears his name.

He had at least some measure of success though. From 1808 until 1810 it was the summer home of Princess Charlotte, daughter of the Prince Regent.

Nearby Felpham for instance has a church with much 13-15th century work and is the burial place of William Hayley, who died in 1820 and was the romantic poet and biographer.

In Vicarage Lane is the charming thatched cottage where visionary poet and painter, William Blake, lived under the patronage of Hayley from 1801 until 1804.

Bolney

Bolney is a Sussex village that has always lived in earshot of the coastal-bound cars and yet remained untouched in its heart.

Bolney is a straightforward place. Through it runs a lane aptly called The Street. And sitting on its foundation of Wealden clay is the Norman church with its fine tower of 1538 and a porch dated 1718.

Indeed it is famous in the county as having the oldest bells in Sussex. The most ancient was cast in 1592 and right up until 1784 Bolney had the only peal of eight.

Not surprisingly Eight Bells became the name of a hostelry in the village. Another less fortunate inn was the Frog and Effett. When Bolney was renowned generations back for its cherry fairs this beerhouse had an equal reputation for the strength of its local brewed beer.

But it fell to a Mr. Courage to put a stop to it all in 1890. Whether he was any connection with the brewing family recent history omits to say. But that he had no sympathies for ale is certain.

He shut the Frog and Effett because he claimed too many of his employees were propping up the bar during working hours and it henceforth became a house of purely domestic nature.

Bolney

There is good reason to describe the style of Bolney Lodge as Regency — because the Prince Regent himself is reputed to have lived there.

If you want to know who to thank for that slip of information it's Bolney Women's Institute. Some years back they were researching for a history of their village, which they finally called rather modestly The Scrap Book.

When they went through the past the ladies found out that the Prince was wont to pop up to Bolney to escape the bustle of the coast. And his equerry, Sir Nelson Ryecroft, wasn't exactly averse to the country jaunts either.

He virtually forced the owners of a property in the village to sell so there were more roofs there for the Royals to shelter under. So certainly Bolney Lodge is Regency.

It appears to have been grafted on the front of an existing older cottage.

But going back a bit, to about 1284 the tenant was one Batholomew de Bolne, who may have succeeded a Robert de Bolneya, mentioned earlier in 1248.

By 1296 principal land owner of the family was a John de Bolneye and he held the manor in the early 1300's.

So it went on down the centuries until the manorial rights lapsed and the Bolneys were left living on in name.

Bosham

The Romans were the first people to occupy the site of Bosham. What is now the fishing and yachting centre stands at the head of Bosham Channel, a creek of Chichester Harbour.

Vespian, commander of the Second Legion, is reputed to have had a camp and a villa at Bosham and on wooded shores there in the 7th century an Irish monk called Dicul built the first church in Sussex and unsuccessfully tried to preach Christianity to the South Saxons.

Later, a monastery was established and Bosham by the 8th century had blossomed into one of the five chief towns in Sussex.

Unfortunately the Danes rather upset things in the 9th century and their marauding bands did great damage to the village. It wasn't entirely a lost chapter as far as Bosham's history was concerned for the famed Canute was subsequently supposed to have built himself a palace and some think that a shore around Bosham could have been the one where he made the famous stand against the waves.

But Canute is not the most historic king with which Bosham is associated. That position must undoubtedly go to Harold, of 1066 date. Two years earlier, in 1064, he sailed from there on the excursion to Normandy that placed him under the dominance of William the Conqueror, an ill-fated expedition recorded in the Bayeux Tapestry.

The king set sail from Quay meadow and nearby is the church — the original of which is represented on the tapestry. Of the original structure, the tower, part of the nave walls and the chancel arch with the western part of the chancel wall have survived.

On the north wall are the remains of a Saxon window and a niche with the mutilated effigy of a lady.

Bramber

You've got to be a mad magpie to collect pipes, says Mr. Anthony Irvine. He should know. He's sitting on a 25,000-piece collection, insured for £300,000 at the House of Pipes in Bramber.

It was a switch from the macabre when stuffed animals went out and the pipes came in.

The animals were in the world-famous Potter collection which had been housed in the museum since 1861.

Like the settings for an Alfred Hitchcock film in miniature, they alternatively fascinated and horrified visitors in a series of detailed tableaux of themes like the Death and Burial of Cock Robin, the Kittens' Wedding and the Guinea Pigs' Cricket Match.

Victorian it certainly was, the freakish and talented work of taxidermist Walter Potter, born and bred in Bramber.

In the early days he kept his collection in a summer house, but as his enthusiasm and the amount of stuffing increased the Bramber museum building was specially built to accommodate the display.

The exhibition was taken over by Mr. Potter's grandson and eventually sold by his widow to Mr. Irvine who in turn took cognisance of his responsibility for a national heritage, refused a £35,000 American offer and did the decent thing by selling it to a Brighton antiques dealer.

Sad to relate stuffed cock robins haven't the same audience attraction they once had.

But pipes have pull. Mr. Irvine has clocked up 15,000 visitors since he took his first puff of Bramber air. He took the bit between his teeth 33 years ago during a visit to Guernsey when he bought a Burmese pipe. It was to form the beginning of a collection which now covers smoking equipment from 150 countries and spans 1,500 years.

Bramber

The Normans built a castle at Bramber, the scant remains of which still stand on a chalk mound on what is the centre of the Adur Valley.

It was sited — like Lewes and Arundel — to command a gap in the South Downs and was built soon after the Conquest by a noble called William de Braose. But like many another fine English fortress it withstood all until the Civil War when, in 1641, it was stormed and wrecked by the Parliamentarians.

The remains today are poignant, evocative and silent.

Further down the street is the architectural gem of St. Mary's, a half-timbered house standing on a site granted to the Knights Templars in the 12th century. In those days Bramber was more than just a stopping off point for coach excursions. It was one of the five Sussex rapes, the name given by the Normans to the administrative areas into which they divided the county.

And the village had a splendid church to match its importance. It was built around 1075 as a chapel for his castle by William de Braose but once again it suffered in the Civil War, when the chancel and transepts were destroyed. But in the late 1700's the tower was restored and since then more restoration has been carried out to match the original Norman style.

Brighton

The Lanes are the remainder of what Brighton was long, long ago — the tiny fishing village of Brighthelmstone.

Brighthelmstone was once virtually nothing but The Lanes. Originally they were paths separating the different gardens and plots of land. Now they are the pedestrian-only footways that separate the proliferating antique shops and their trendy boutique neighbours.

But they are still in the cosy cluster of buildings that once housed the fisherfolk who were Brighton's first residents. Over the years, of course, fishermen and their families made way for other trades. Early 19th-century directories show that in Middle Street there was a "coal merchant and a cow-keeper," which today would hardly seem a straight-forward commercial combination.

Later were to come the boot and shoe makers, who in time had the largest amount of shops and work rooms in The Lanes — followed closely by the cabinet makers, bakers and — to keep the wheels of industry turning with a fluid motion — the small taverns and beer shops.

Brighton

The Royal Pavilion is the most bizarre architectural fantasy ever to grace England's green land.

The onion domes and minarets have been Brighton's most famous landmark throughout the world. Unique is not a word to use lightly. But if anything ever deserved the description, it is the Pavilion.

It is inseparably linked with the Prince Regent. He first came to Brighton in 1783 to get away from his over-strict father, fell in love with the town and later took a house where the pavilion's music room now stands. After marrying Mrs. Fitzherbert in 1785, he took another house in the Steine — the one destined to be transformed into the Pavilion.

It was subsequently rebuilt under architect Henry Holland and finished in 1787. This building formed the nucleus of the present pavilion. The green painted, tent-shaped canopies were added to the balconies during the years 1801 to 1804. At this time also two new oval-shaped rooms were added and the whole interior was given its Chinese flavour.

Improvements under Nash began in 1815. The banqueting and music rooms were added in 1817 and the Pavilion finished about 1820. From the beginning of the building to the end of the reign of its owner, the overall bill was more than £500,000.

The Octagon entrance hall gives the first interior taste of things to come in the Pavilion. It has the original brass fireplace, and a tented ceiling. Among furniture lent by the Queen are a pair of 18th century Chinese cabinets, two beautiful enamelled bronze incense burners and a pair of elbow chairs made for this room.

Restorations in the vestibule in 1962 removed many layers of old paint and varnish. The chandelier for 17 lights was lent by the Queen. Just one item on display here: a pair of Sevres vases.

Brighton

Lewes Crescent, Brighton, dates from the very beginning of the Kemp Town estate. It was laid out from 1823 to 1828 as the first joint work of Amon Wilds and C. A. Busby. It's the natural complement in the east to Brunswick Square and Adelaide Crescent in the west at Hove.

Among houses at Lewes Crescent is one once occupied by the crescent's builder, Thomas Cubitt. To the north — in Sussex Square — is the house at No. 22 where Kemp Town's virtual founder, Thomas Read Kemp, lived.

Kemp was the member of a Lewes family. His father had been the constituency's MP and also High Sheriff of Sussex. He was a joint lord of the then manor of Brighton and his son eventually assumed the title.

Kemp junior became a Member of Parliament in 1823, left England in 1837 and died in 1844. But not before starting with his architects Wilds and Busby the crescent and terraces that have always been the contrasting heart of a Kemp Town that in later years found a reputation for being more racy.

The beauty of Lewes Crescent lies in the balance of its composition and its use of the gentle hill sloping down to the sea. At the height of its fame the wealthy and famous people who lived there had no trouble running the gauntlet of South Coast traffic as today. They took their dip when courageous enough after reaching the sea from a tunnel which led from square to beach.

And famous visitors and residents certainly were frequent along this stretch of Brighton's front. No. 1 at the west end — with the adjoining house at 14 Chichester Terrace — was the home from 1828 until his death in 1858 of the sixth Duke of Devonshire. Here he entertained notable people who included William IV and the Austrian Chancellor Prince Metternich.

Brighton

The last beadle of Brighton lived in the pretty cottage opposite St. Nicolas Church, Dyke Road.

The cottage which was built in 1801, was renamed Shelleys, after William Shelley, the short ginger-bearded beadle who lived there and was able to go to the church by way of the underground passage which runs from Shelley's cellar to the basement rooms below the church. It is blocked up now, but was thought to have been used by the beadle for smuggling.

The beadle of a parish brought to the notice of the vicar any poor and needy folk. He also arranged baptisms, marriages and christenings because the vicar in those days was too grand to do such things. The sermons lasted for two hours sometimes and it was the duty of the beadle to poke anyone in the back with his staff if he caught them snoozing.

The red-haired and red-bearded Shelley is mentioned in the deeds of the cottage. This is what it says: "A goodly parcel of sheep-grazing ground in the church furlong of St. Nicholas, whereupon to build a goodly cottage for Master William Shelley, beadle of St. Nicholas, for the sum of £120." Dated December, 1821.

William Shelley lived there until he died on the 6th July, 1872.

In 1820 Mount Zion Place was called Sion Hill, and there were tiny shops and cottages all down the hill towards Church Street; a grocer, a tea dealer, a tailor, an eating house and a man named Nathan Smith who invented an air pump for extracting gout, a disease caused by chalky substance in the joints.

Brighton

In 1885, where Roedean School stands now at the termination of the Sussex Downland Valley from which it takes its name, sheep grazed on the short, springy turf.

Today the name Roedean is synonymous throughout the world with the best of girls' education in the best of British traditions. But as with all things of worth in society, Roedean owes its existence to the far-sighted idealism and perception of remarkable people.

In this case it was the sisters Penelope, Dorothy, and Millicent Lawrence. They were of that rarest breed of staunch and self-determined Victorian women whose strength did not obscure their femininity and whose power lay in their resolve and determination.

Teachers in their own right, the three of them made their historic beginning in a house at No. 25 Lewes Crescent in 1885. It accommodated 15 girls but barely a year after this first venture an increasing number of pupils led the sisters to open No. 3 Arundel Terrace.

By 1887 still another house was needed and No. 26 Lewes Crescent was taken, openings being made into No. 25, with lodgings at No. 37 Chesham Road serving as a sanatorium.

Eventually the school moved to several converted houses in Sussex Square for the intermediate stage of its history.

The aim, it said, was to give a thorough education, physical, intellectual and moral. The fees were to be £126 per annum, exclusive of solo-singing, piano, violin, riding and dancing.

In those early days the establishment was known as Wimbledon House School and by the early 1890's it had 90 pupils.

But the inevitable was happening. Roedean's very success was causing it growing-pains that had to be dealt with. So it was that the founders moved to their present famous site overlooking the English Channel.

The land was purchased from the Marquess of Abergavenny and the first Downland turf was turned on March 16, 1897, with the school being given a holiday to mark the occasion.

Brighton

Hangleton Manor is the oldest house in Brighton and Hove. Estimates put an erection date at between 1540 and 1560 and they point to the left hand side of the main door and two carved Norman stones traced to Lewes Priory, itself demolished in 1537.

The largest oak beam in the manor is 12in. square and more than 25ft. long. Some more historical guesswork estimates that to have grown that size would have taken about 300 years — and so presumably the oak must have started to sprout around 1250.

But you can see your way to more than just heavy beams in the manor. There are more than 1,000 panels of glass set into walls that are up to four feet thick in places.

When William the Conqueror held sway, the grounds of Hangleton Manor were about 1,200 acres and, of course, Hangleton appears in the Domesday Book when the area was occupied by a man called Azor.

It wasn't too long before the Poynings family owned Hangleton — 1291 to be precise. They possessed it until 1446 and from then on the manor comes through history and owners, with the Sackville family term ending after owning the freehold for 320 years.

It was subsequently opened as a hotel in later years but some of the visitors were vandals who achieved what the years had failed — the building's near ruin.

But it is as a non-residential hotel that it was restored to its former glory, even though the requisite ghost stories remain.

Brighton

It was one Mr. John Willing to whom Brighton owes the debt or otherwise of the Clock Tower. He was a wealthy local advertising contractor in his seventies when he decided that Brighton should have an item of note to celebrate the first jubilee of Queen Victoria.

The item turned out to be the Clock Tower, all 75 immovable towering feet of it. Work started in January 1888. By summer it was completed — with a speed that is an ironic reflection of the years spent trying to be rid of it. The cost? A mere £2,000.

It was designed by an architect called John Johnson. And as top deck bus passengers would note if they were to look further than the French students who cluster round the Clock Tower in summer, he managed to avoid some of the usual spiky Gothic Victorian creations and instead achieved something almost baroque in its classical style.

The tower is a square white stone structure with a red granite base on the four sides of which are porticoes and Corinthian columns and pediments enclosing medallion portraits in coloured mosaic of Victoria, Albert and others.

What even top deck passengers can't see is the gilded dome which survives the exhaust fumes high above the tower. At one time it was controlled by direct electrical communication from Greenwich Observatory and the ball rose by hydraulic power and fell precisely every hour.

Brighton

St Peter's Church has been the parish church of Brighton since 1873. It stands between the milling traffic on the Lewes and London roads. It is and always has been considered one of the finest churches built in England during the early stages of the Gothic revival.

But then perhaps the architect was more than usually talented. He was in fact Charles Barry, later Sir Charles Barry, designer of Hurstpierpoint church and also the Houses of Parliament.

When St. Peter's was consecrated in 1828 he was 28-years-old and he was commissioned for the work after a public competition to find the best architect.

The church took four years to build and cost £16,000. But it was built of Purbeck stone and down the years that was to cause trouble.

Sir Charles himself was one of the first to recognise his mistake. The stone was ideal for the highly ornamental exterior of the building but even a few years after completion began to show signs of erosion by saltladen winds from the sea.

But generous well wishers down the years have always footed the bill for keeping the stone fabric of the church in good repair and £20,000 recently raised now has the Purbeck stone largely erosion-proof.

A staggering sum when compared with church expenditure at earlier stages of its history. In 1874 a £3,000 plan to alter and enlarge the church was agreed and in 1876 St. Peter's reopened with many alterations and additions.

A year later a fine new font was used for the first time — unusual for its size and the bargain bill of only £4,000 that accompanied it.

The font was in memory of the Rev. Thomas Cooke, first incumbent of St. Peters, and a gentleman who stayed there for 50 years.

The year 1910 saw a new organ, although it took until 1966 before it was completed with a fine oak case to embellish its musical charm.

St. Peter's traditional Yuletide gesture for home going motorists as they speed out of Brighton is the illuminated Christmas tree that stands in front of the church doors.

There have been hopes in the past that St. Peter's might become the cathedral of a new diocese in Sussex. So far they haven't been realised.

In the eyes of many this stately church already is the Cathedral of Brighton.

Brighton

No building of the architectural splendour of Brighton's Royal Pavilion could have a more impressive entrance than its North Gate.

It towers above the pavement and provides a splendid foretaste of the Royal Palace to come.

Yet it is William IV and not George IV we have to thank for the North Gate.

He had it erected in 1832 and it was an acknowledgement of the grandeur he recognised the Pavilion commanded.

Man in charge of the building operations was a Joseph Good, Clerk of Works to the Tower and Royal Mint and afterwards in charge of Kensington Palace.

His inspiration was a model made by Pavilion architect Nash before he left Brighton in disgust at the cost of King George's seaside extravaganza.

Down the years the North Gate has changed very little from the building that was originally intended to set the seal on the Pavilion as a whole.

It is constructed with a combination of Bath and Portland stone, which also combines a solid appearance with a graceful line needed to enhance the onion-domed architecture of the Pavilion.

And on more than one occasion its appearance has been transformed by the trappings of celebration. When Queen Victoria came to Brighton only four months after her accession — on October 4, 1837, the North Gate was bedecked with flags and trappings and turned into a triumphal archway of flowers.

Brighton

Brighton College came into being as a public school in 1845. But like many other momentous starts, it was followed by a slow and gradual growth.

The first buildings were in Lion House, Portland Place, plus three neighbouring houses for boarders and another property in Upper Rock Gardens for a chapel. The first lessons were given on January 26, 1847.

Soon after, in 1848, the College bought its present Eastern Road site and builders Wizden and Anscombe put up the first building — at a breath-taking cost of £5,716.

They were days of obvious cash awareness too, because in 1854 the School House, which was the headmaster's residence and a boarding house, was built at the head's own expense. It was rented to successive principals until the college stepped in as purchaser in 1873.

In subsequent years development came along at a steady rate:

The earliest part of the chapel was erected in 1859 with the 200 pupil level being passed in 1863.

Headmaster Dawson's arrival in 1906 saw a further period of great expansion with six new boarding houses and a fully fledged prep school. There had been a junior department ever since 1845!

The depression years brought a classroom contraction but World War II was no deterrent. School policy was to stay open, which it did through thick and thin, even with a considerably reduced number of boys and staff.

Even girls as pupils in the sixth form have been successfully incorporated and now, with the number of pupils standing at 430 and fees at £1,470 per annum for senior boarders and £975 for senior day boys the College Development Fund are considering relocatable buildings.

Brighton

The Dome is that friendly Brighton building built as a stable but where horses have long since been moved out in favour of 2,000-plus seats, orchestras, pop groups, operettas and union conferences.

It is doubtful whether any horse-lovers ever built their equestrian friends a home to rival The Dome in architecture and luxury. This decidedly individual building goes right back to the beginning of Regency Brighton. It was started in 1803 by William Porden, who had succeeded Holland as royal architect.

The Corn Exchange dates from the same time and was used as a royal riding school. Porden used for both the same Islamic style of architecture for which the Dome and the royal Pavillion have become so famous.

The circular Dome had stable accommodation for 44 horses and the upper floor was taken up with storage space for harnesses and saddle rooms. Light came from a large glass dome that topped the roof, which was a steep 65ft. from the ground. To keep the horses well watered, a drinking fountain once stood in the centre of the floor. The Dome was purchased by the town along with the Pavilion estate in 1850 and was converted into a concert hall by 1867. From 1914 to 1930 it was used as a military hospital and in 1935 its interior was remodelled to convert it into the social and cultural centre it has become today.

Burpham

The beautiful village of Burpham is tucked away on the banks of the River Arun.

After leaving Arundel and its castle, you reach it via a pleasantly winding lane that forks off the Brighton Road just as it starts to climb out of the valley in which Arundel lies.

Or if you really feel energetic there's a footpath that will take you along the river and eventually over a large earthwork surrounded by trees.

This is the site of a Saxon burgh or fortified township, one of the many thought to have been set up by Alfred the Great to ward off attacks by Danes.

Once in the quiet of Burpham itself you'll find a sympathetically restored 12th and 13th century church.

It has a late Norman nave with unusual piers and an arcade of chalk with carved capitals and zigzag mouldings.

They've been worshipping here for a long time, as the 14th century oak seats in the nave testify.

But when you've sat there and absorbed the quiet calm of this peaceful village try the path which goes north of the church on the east of the Arun to the ridge on which North Stoke stands, with a Georgian manor house and a 12th century church.

If you're still feeling fresh you can go further by footpath across the Downs all the way to Amberley and Storrington.

Burwash

Burwash must for ever remain one of the most beautiful villages in Sussex. It was also for many years the home of that greatest of British authors, Rudyard Kipling.

From 1902 until his death in 1936 he lived here in Batemans, which surely, too, must rank as one of the loveliest small houses in the county and which was bequeathed to the National Trust by Mrs. Kipling in 1940.

Batemans was built in 1634 for a local iron master. Its stone built walls shelter a veritable wealth of Kipling articles and the countryside around is intimately described in Puck of Pook's Hill and Rewards and Fairies.

Burwash itself was rich in more than one way during the years gone by. In the 15th and 16th centuries it was one of the most flourishing centres of the Sussex iron industry. This helps account for the wealth of charming houses and cottages lining its streets.

The village church was rebuilt in 1856 but still incorporates the Norman tower, the wide 13th century chancel arch and the nave arcades.

In the east end of the south aisle is a 14th century Sussex iron grave slab with a Lombardic inscription to "Jhone Colins," one of a family of local iron founders. It forms the oldest example of this kind of work in Sussex.

Burwash is naturally the type of place to inspire and in a literary context it didn't start with Kipling.

The village has had at least two notable literary rectors, James Hurdis, who was a poet and who was here from 1788 until 1791 and J. Coker Egerton, author of Sussex Folk and Sussex Ways, who was in residence from 1867 until 1888.

Along the ridge in Burwash Common history is thick with the memories of less notable people. The area was notorious in the 18th century for its gangs of smugglers and sheep stealers.

But now they and their ill deeds have gone, leaving the beauty and the echoes of Kipling to be a source of pleasure to the appreciative for ever.

Batemans is open to the public during the summer.

Bury

Bury is a secluded West Sussex village where the saga of author John Galsworthy unfolded when he lived there in Bury House from 1926 to 1933.

It's also the place where literary tradition has it that Peter Pan's creator, Sir James Barrie, was more than unusually afraid of the dark.

In those days Bury had to generate its own electricity, and at Bury House they had a generator to bring light and current into their lives.

It worked well until Barrie came to visit. For he was scared stiff of the dark and used to insist on a bedroom light burning all night — which meant that the generator constantly overheated.

But Galsworthy was nothing but kindness exemplified. Rather than embarrass his friend or ask him to pass the night with a paraffin lamp by his bedside he quietly had a second generator installed to supply comforting nocturnal illumination.

It was at Bury that Galsworthy completed the Forsyte Saga and certainly the Downland countryside through which he used to take an early morning ride was inspirational.

The village lies on the edge of the Arun Valley. It is an area rich in history, from nearby Bignor with its exquisite Roman villa, across the Arun to Amberley and the gaunt walls of its castle.

Bury church was built between 1200 and 1250 of flint, stone and chalk. The register dates back to 1560 and there is a 15th century holy water stoup in an outside wall.

A shingled oak spire was added to the building in 1603.

The crowning glory of the area is Bury Hill, with extensive and sweeping views down the Arun Valley from a 450ft. summit.

Galsworthy's wife Ada thought so too. She lived for 22 years after he died in 1933 and then her ashes were scattered on the top of Bury Hill.

Chailey

Chailey is a long strip of mellow, fruitful countryside which stretches inland from Lewes. Chailey North Common is said to mark the exact centre of the whole county. And from here you can enjoy unrivalled views of the Downs that stretch in sight from Eastbourne through the landmarks of Firle, Caburn and Ditchling Beacon to beyond Bignor Hill.

The North Common is a bracken, heath and pasture refuge which boasts rare plants and unusual birds and insects. Nearby is the famous Chailey Heritage, a renowned centre where crippled children are taught how to overcome their handicaps. It dates back to 1903 when it was founded by Dame Grace Kimmins.

Chailey itself is split into three parts. The common with its scattered houses and King's Head Inn is one. South Chailey is another. But the real centre is Chailey Green, which was once the original village and which still has its parish church and resplendent cedar tree.

Then, of course, Chailey has the busy A275 bearing traffic from the coast. But its attraction hasn't been blotted out in motor car exhaust fumes. The authentic atmosphere of rural Sussex countryside is nothing but hardy. And it needs to be.

Chelwood Gate

There couldn't have been a nicer place for Super Mac to have retreated to after the rigours of his political life than the verdant and restful acres of his house at Birch Grove.

As the Rt. Hon. Harold Macmillan, head of the family publishing firm, Prime Minister and First Lord of the Treasury from 1957 until 1963, he then swapped the lobbies and galleries of Westminster for daffodil beds and the peaceful quiet of rolling countryside at Chelwood Gate, in the heartland of Sussex.

It was his father who made it all possible. He first espied this corner of the county back in 1906 and purchased a house occupying the site then. But by 1923 the original building had outgrown its usefulness and the Macmillans decided on a replacement.

In that year the present Birch Grove House was started and in 1926 the last brick and finishing touches were laid to what has been the family home ever since.

They couldn't have chosen a part of Sussex with more historical connections.

Ashdown Forest is all that remains of those great green swathes, once the hunting ranges of knights and nobles.

But what the village used to be is indicated by a 1693 map of the Ashdown Forest Conservators, which showed 6,400 acres at Ashdown Forest marked over for the use of commoners, and Chelwood Gate clearly indicated as an entrance to its green open spaces.

Modern Chelwood Gate is a scattered place with many of the older buildings made of amber sandstone quarried locally by local craftsmen.

But today there isn't a character of history, from the Romans to John of Gaunt, who ranks as a bigger attraction than Chelwood Gate's present famous citizen.

He leads a quiet life walking in some of the finest private gardens for their size in Sussex. Before Lady Dorothy died in 1966 these and the ground floor were open for occasional visiting.

Now just the gardens are open at selected times in the spring, and the daffodil display ranks as one of the South's finest.

Chelwood Gate

Inside Chelworth House, Chelwood Gate, Sussex, resides a holder of the Golden Cross of Merit, Polonia, Poland, a commodore of the Order of the Phoenix, Greece, and the Order of the Cedar, Lebanon. He's also a very keen gardener.

They all have the one thing in common — the personage of Lord Chelwood of Lewes, better known as Sir Tufton Beamish, former MP for Lewes, man of action, politician and author.

Better known is the right phrase, too, for people in the Lewes area. Sir Tufton represented the constituency from 1945 until 1974 and ended his years as a parliamentarian by being a member of the European Parliament in Strasbourg.

When his father left the Navy as the youngest rear-admiral and bought Chelworth House in 1922 it was with one thing in mind — to stand for the Lewes constituency.

The family couldn't have chosen a better strategic Sussex vantage point or Sir Tufton a better source from which to take his title than Chelwood.

Nobody knows better about Sussex history than Lord Chelwood. Among publications that distinguishes him as a member of the Society of Authors is a famous and authoritative county book, Battle Royal, an account for the 700th anniversary of Simon de Montfort's struggle against Henry III and the famous Battle of Lewes that led directly to the setting up of the English Parliament.

The views are worth looking at. They stretch right across the county to Chanctonbury Ring and to Beachy Head in the opposite direction. The other view is the one lucky summer visitors have of inspecting Lord Chelwood's prowess as a gardener on the occasional days when the grounds are open for charity.

The aim has been informality, blending rhododendrons, azaleas and camellias with the natural vegetation of Ashdown Forest.

Chelwood Gate

Once John of Gaunt had a hunting lodge nearby. And once Chelwood Gate really was the gateway to the great Forest of Anderida.

Chelwood Gate now leads only to Ashdown Forest, the last breezy moorland to remind us of the tree-covered acres where royal families from Roman times had hunted.

Today it is a scattered place, centring round a long high street and residing in the memories of historic associations.

A 1693 map of the Ashdown Forest Conservators shows 6,400 acres of land at Ashdown Forest marked over for the use of commoners and Chelwood Gate as a clearly marked entrance to its green open spaces.

The village has blended the new with the old down the centuries. Of the more mature buildings many of them are made of amberstone sandstone quarried in times past locally and by local craftsmen.

A more recent arrival is the University of Sussex. They have an outpost at the Isle of Thorns. Once this was the only piece of hard land in an area surrounded by waterlogged and boggy forest valleys.

Some impromptu reclamation in the area helped it later to become a farm which was taken over by the Manor Charitable Trust after the First World War and made into a 120-acre holiday camp for the less fortunate lads from London.

The youngsters there today are more qualified in all respects. Sussex University came to the Isle of Thorns in 1964 and built a centre called the White House for short course study.

What is still a gateway village to some of the best Sussex wide open spaces has also become, for some, a new gateway to learning.

Chichester

Chichester is one of the finest and most impressive cities in Sussex, England and Europe.

The Romans founded the modern city of Chichester with a city of their own called Regnum or Noviomagus.

It only wants an instant realisation of how the four main streets cross so neatly in right angles to realise that the Romans must have been responsible for basic pioneering town planning like that.

Before them had been the Belgae, anything but sophisticated invaders from Northern France, whose forays into Sussex took them to the Chichester region around the first century BC.

Before the Roman legions came ashore they cemented an alliance of local tribes and elected as their chieftain Cogidubnus, the man who eventually went over to the conquerors and acquired for himself the now world-famous palace of Fishbourne just outside the city.

But the Romans went. Chichester stayed prosperous but static for a few centuries and it wasn't until 1075, when it became the seat of a bishopric, that the second and continuing phase of its history commenced.

But to get back to the majestic cathedral, which is the focal point of the living architectural exhibition piece that is Chichester. The first part of it was consecrated in 1108. Building was started after his consecration in 1091 by Bishop Ralph de Luffa.

Chichester

The City Cross in Chichester stands in the middle of this most beautiful of Sussex communities.

It remains the finest example of an English market cross in the country and Chichester's proudest historic possession after the cathedral.

It was built in 1500 by Bishop Edward Storey as a shelter for people coming in from the surrounding rural areas to sell their wares on market day.

Now it stands at the junction of the city's four main shopping streets. Then it stood at the centre of a wide market which some say stretched as far north as Crane Street and as far east as St. Martin's Street.

Here the poor and the peasants gradually came to occupy the same selling spaces each week and eventually began to regard plots as being privileged for their families.

Eventually pitches were put up for sale — even though the bishop wished the Cross to remain for ever the centre of a free market place.

Chichester

Time must have weighed heavily on the hands of Roman infantrymen thousands of miles from home after they had pacified the ancient Britons.

While squatting on the mosaic waiting for action they engaged in the noble game of dice throwing. We know because dice sets turned up at Regnum, or Noviomagus, or Chichester as it is known to us, on the site of the original Old Cross Hotel in North Street.

When a new building was put up in 1924 its Roman remains in the cellars were excavated.

The old hotel dated back many centuries but eventually fell a victim to woodworm and other voracious bugs before being put out of its misery.

The new building which went up in its place is as near a copy of the original as could be imagined, oak beams allowing.

The first performers on the historical stage of Chichester were the Belgae, invaders from Northern France, who reached the Sussex coast around the middle of the first century BC.

They built themselves the pioneer town of Noviomagus which means "new city on the plain," near the head of what was then a navigable harbour.

But when the Romans came chief Cognibudnus changed sides, co-operated and was made a local king and legate by the Emperor Claudius.

Soon after, Chichester became Roman Regnum.

Chilgrove

You journey through Chilgrove in almost seconds. Past the long green and the old manor house. Past the White Horse Inn where the licensee says they attract loads of weekend customers.

The population has stayed at around 100. So hamlet is the word to describe the tiny community.

But small in population though it may be, Chilgrove figures large in another sense — historically. For in 1963 a farmer was ploughing a field at nearby Brick Kiln Farm on the Westdean estate when he uncovered a Roman column that once supported the verandah of a villa.

It was a find which has made Chilgrove one of the most important archaeological sites in West Sussex. Under the supervision of Mr. Alec Down an excavation committee attached to the Chichester Civic Society have now uncovered separate villas.

Both date back to the late 1st century AD. The first has been completely excavated while work on the second still continues. But already it has been established that it is half the size of the now famous Fishbourne Palace further south.

The patient work of Mr. Down and his team established that both were destroyed by fire in the late 4th c entury, the second one about ten years after the first, and despite that they were used for a squatting type of accommodation after that.

Clayton

Artistic vandals can have their virtues, even if it's hard to appreciate at the time.

Such vandal stepped forth with a major lack of aesthetic appreciation and a pot of red paint in St. John the Baptist Church at Clayton some time during the Reformation.

In anything but an old master fashion he slapped an unconscious preservative coat over a set of 12th century wall paintings that make the church unique in England.

For 300 years the Last Judgement paintings, among the finest and earliest of their type in the country, lay hidden under their red covering, itself probably intended to provide a plain background for the rood. It was only in 1893 that the famous Clayton murals saw the light again.

It is thought they were the work of monks from the Cluniac Priory of St. Pancras at Lewes, owners of St. John's.

Some think the paintings are of a different style and perhaps date back to Saxon times.

But of uncertain derivation or no, the historic nature of the murals is not in question. They cover the north, east and south walls of the nave and they are in vivid and lively colours.

Experts have dated them at about 1150 and say they were painted on while plaster was still wet.

Restoration work proper got under way in 1963.

They now form the chief attrction in a distinctively Sussex church that has always concealed a long history behind an unpretentious exterior.

Cocking

In the Domesday Book they called Cocking by the name of Cochinges. In some respects the name is one of the few things that has changed with the centuries at this delightful flinty village which nestles at the foot of the Downs on the main road from Midhurst to Chichester.

There is no better start for a walk over this wooded section of the Downs than Cocking. The parish church is in the Norman and decorated styles, with three ancient bells in its tower.

In the nave there is a mural painting dated 1220 and the register commences in 1558.

Although in part restored, the church has three old and possibly original tie-beams supporting the nave roof and a 13th century south aisle with a contemporary aumbry. The north aisle and arcade were added in 1865.

In 1357 the parish was owned by Richard Fitzalan, the 9th Earl of Arundel, and it stayed in his family until its transfer in the reign of Elizabeth to Sir Anthony Browne, the first Viscount Montagu.

Cowfold

Brook Farm House at Cowfold was built by a Sussex iron master in 1707. He operated his hammer pond industry in the Mannings Heath area.

Its seven bedrooms are under a Horsham slab roof and behind walls of local stone. Many of its timbers came from ancient warships — brought, possibly, from ship building yards in the New Forest.

Research has shown that the original iron master of Cowfold probably sent many of the ship fittings his men manufactured by barge and inland waterway to the yards

The timbers came back to Sussex by way of return cargoes from warships that were being broken up.

They helped make for a stout house. It now stands in a 70-acre estate.

Cowfold

Cowfold stands at the junction of the A272 and the A281 road from the South Coast to Horsham.

Here is St. Hugh's Charterhouse Monastery, lying a mile or so south from the community centre. It was built at the end of the last century and took nearly 600 men six years to complete. It is one of the biggest in the country and its cloisters at nearly a mile long are thought to be among the world's biggest. As an order the Carthusian is strict. All monks are vegetarian and they live a life of silent meditation.

The village church of Cowfold has seen a different kind of worshipper through the years. It was built in 1272 and is as typical as an English country church could be. The tower was added in the 15th century.

Here can be seen on application one of the finest brasses in the country. It is the 1433 Nelond Brass, which commemorates Thomas Nelond, prior of the Cluniad Abbey of St. Pancras at Lewes. He died in 1429 but this piece of craftsmanship ensures that he is never quite forgotten.

Also never to be forgotten are the economics of the church's splendid font, built in 1471. The receipt for it shows that the iron and lock cost 6d; carriage of the stone was 8d; lime fetched all of 4d and the fetching of that in turn totalled 1d. For his part in the production the stonemason was paid 5s for a work that has given centuries of service.

Crawley

The charming country house of the Ancient Priors at Crawley was built in 1150 and was a prior's house from where a gentleman of the church used to step forth to take care of the religious needs of Crawley's forerunners.

It wasn't always to remain so. Times and their demands changed and it seems likely that by Cromwell the priors had been forced out of the property during repressions that were waged against the established church. Along with them went the deeds to the property, which were lost at the same time.

Some say that Ancient Priors had seen a changed usage before even then. They favour the history that has Henry VIII and Anne Boleyn riding out from the clamour of London and into the greenery of Sussex to stay at the house for a night in the country.

Certainly they'd have been in for a shock today, when Ancient Priors is isolated like some island of the past in Crawley High Street.

It was first converted into a cafe and sweetshop in 1937. In 1934 it was an estage agents, and further back still there was a restoration in 1927 and an extension in the early days of 1440.

The elements have possibly helped wipe out evidence that might have thrown more light on the early years. Once there was a cellar that went deep into the earth under the ancient timbers.

But floods following the diversion of a water course some 23 years back swamped this particular part of Crawley and the cellars disappeared in a subsequent tide of in-filling concrete.

Cuckfield

Cuckfield lies almost northwards as the crow flies from Brighton and is the centre of an administrative area which embraces its neighbour, Haywards Heath.

Cuckfield's history — and it goes back at least to 1254 when it was granted a charter — is that of a former market town, with all the rural charm and bustle such communities displayed.

The main street still reflects the past. In 1876 Henry Kingsley, the novelist and the younger brother of Charles Kingsley, died at a cottage called Attrees, a 17th century half-timbered residence at the top of the hill.

North of the parish church is the former grammar school — founded in 1521. What's left today is largely a 17th century building, although it has been extensively modified through the years. But it still has an original fireplace and oak beams.

In a lane past the King's Head pub is another time-matured building, Ockenden Manor. It dates partly from the 16th century.

The church was rebuilt about 1250 on the foundations of a Norman building. It has a 13th century tower and a 15th century roof, distinctive for its paintings and bosses carrying the arms of the Nevills, once lords of the manor.

Cuckfield

Cuckfield Park is a splendid Elizabethan house built by a Sussex ironmaster.

It was later owned by the Sergison family and they had a macabre habit of placing their dead in the gatehouse the previous day and night before burial — and then setting off on the final torchlight journey to the parish church as the clock struck midnight.

The mourners had to pass what was called the Doom Tree, which was supposed to have dropped a branch as a mark of respect.

The Sergison family owned Cuckfield Park for nearly 270 years. Charles Sergison was a high up in the Admiralty, following Samuel Pepys as Commissioner of the Navy and Clerk of the Accounts. It was a job he held through three reigns.

After the last war the house became a college of domestic science when it was sold by descendants of the first Charles Sergison. Mr. Holt moved in after the college closed in 1972.

The house has many interesting features spanning the periods, including an Elizabethan screen and plaster ceiling, 16th and 17th century panelling, richly carved fireplaces with original firebacks and an overmantel attributed to the School of Grinling Gibbons.

Ditchling Village

Ditchling is the artist's village of Sussex. But you don't necessarily have to have an artist's eye for beauty to be able to appreciate all the charms and the atmosphere of rural tranquility which make this such a desirable place.

Ditchling stands on a hummock of the greensand ridge dominated by Ditchling Beacon, one of the highest points of the lofty South Downs.

A Roman road once ran from east to west, north of crossroads around which the village sprung up. Tradition has it too that there was once a royal park in the district, where Edward II kept a stud of horses when he was Prince of Wales. And possible evidence of this were the remnants of a manor house found here during the 19th century.

Probably the most spectacular of the weathered, warm houses of which the centre of Ditchling consists is yet another Anne of Cleves' House. This particular one is a rambling 16th century mansion of brick and half-timber work and was one of many manor houses given by Henry VIII to his divorced fourth wife.

But like so many of the other Anne of Cleves' Houses, there is no evidence to show that the lady herself actually lived here.

Eastbourne

Eastbourne is a county borough, one of the largest communities in Sussex and also one of the most select of coastal resorts.

But up until the mid-19th century modern Eastbourne as such hardly existed. In those days the area was merely three separate hamlets, the oldest being a settlement called by the name that subsequently stuck — East Bourne.

There was another hamlet called South Bourne lying back from the sea, and nearer the shore a group of fishermen's cottages called Sea Houses.

Centuries ago the Romans had lived hereabouts. Once the remains of a Roman country house were found north-east of the pier. But they were built over and the Eastbourne that has grown up with its compressed history owes its development and prosperity largely to the second Duke of Devonshire, the principal Eastbourne land-owner of his day.

Eastbourne has a stylish front of terraced promenades that one way ends in the greenery of Princes Park and goes onwards to the shingle banks called the Crumbles and Pevensey Bay.

In the other direction lies the splendour of Beachy Head and the Old Town where links with the past are stronger.

Eastbourne

You've heard of a quick pint giving you an equally quick lift. Well there's a pub in Eastbourne where it's the pint itself that gets the lift — by virtue of a cellar in the roof. The conventional brewery world is turned upside down at the Prince Albert in Eastbourne High Street. The topsy turvy situation goes back to times when the pub was built in 1937. It was constructed immediately behind a much older pub knocked down when the Prince Albert was finished. Designer Mr. Hugh Ford turned the building into a mock Tudor creation.

But when it came to interior installations central heating requirements clashed with cellar needs. Warmth won. The heating plant went downstairs and the beer hit the roof.

Licensee Mr. Jim Pinn is fond of his unusual beer supply. For a start, when you pull a pint you don't have to pull so hard. And the beer needs less gas than the underground variety to reach bar level.

Draymen aren't so keen though. The Prince Albert is one place where they have to haul themselves and the beer up instead of lowering to the depths.

It all gives another dimension to Mr. Pinn's career as a publican. He has been at the Prince Albert for 21 years. Before that he and his family ran the Kings Arms at Eastbourne for 38 years. So it's almost natural that he has a trade hobby — collecting corkscrews.

East Dean

East Dean is one of those refreshing Sussex villages not spoiled by a pretty appearance.

Not that this hamlet in the Lavant Valley is without charm. Simply that it still retains the atmosphere of a place where people both work and live rather than being a community frozen in picture postcard scenic beauty.

First of all, don't confuse this East Dean with the one near Eastbourne. The West Sussex village lies in an area that once used to be part of the Goodwood estate and was owned by the Dukes of Richmond.

Its flint houses and streets are nearer farmers' fields than the new housing developments and road highways.

Look hard enough and you'll see faint lines which indicate where prehistoric fields used to be long ago.

The other part of East Dean's atmosphere comes from the thickly wooded Downs round-about, carefully nurtured and protected by the Forestry Commission.

But not many of the trees there are as old as the village church. It dates back to 1150, and has a simple interior of oak beams and white washed walls.

And the way in is via history too — through an arch main doorway that was built around 1200.

East Dean

East Dean nestles just behind that splendid part of the Sussex coastline which comes to a noble climax at Beachy Head.

It lies in a valley which in summer is fresh with green beauty but which in winter has certain notoriety with motorists, because East Dean is invariably the first place at which the main Brighton to Eastbourne road becomes blocked during heavy snowfalls.

The older part of the hamlet is scattered around the side of the valley and exists happily with the newer homes of Eastbourne which are mushrooming on the hillside north of the main road.

The richness of the countryside is pleasantly contrasted by the simple yet interesting church. It has a late Norman nave, a chancel of about 1190 and Norman — or possibly Saxon — tower.

Built into the north wall of the nave are the remains of the tower arch and of a supporting arch in which Norman stones have been re-used.

Here too is a damaged grave-slab of about 1300 carved with a cross and the arms of the Bardolf family of Birling. In a niche in the wall is a 13th century chalice and paten found in the grave of a priest outside the chancel.

More testimony to centuries of prayer comes with a carved oak pulpit and sounding-board dated 1623. The nave and chancel also retain their original 15th century roofs.

At East Dean the nearness of the sea and the spectacular stretch of Sussex coast is easily felt. The road which follows the valley down to the sea leads to Birling Gap, the only break in the white cliffs between Holywell and Cuckmere Haven.

The whole area is a ramblers' paradise and a corner of Sussex where the grandeur of scenic beauty has not yet been marred by man.

East Grinstead

East Grinstead is a country market town that dates back to the 12th century. Then it was called Grenestede but by 1271 it was changed to Estgrenested to differentiate between it and the village of West Grinstead, near Horsham.

The name itself means "green place," and East Grinstead was once such a verdant clearing when Ashdown Forest really was what it is still called.

At the western end is Judges' Terrace and a building that was an assize court until 1799, and nearby is the Dorset Arms, which once used to reverberate with the noise of horses' hooves as coach passengers stopped off on their journey for refreshment.

The parish church occupies the site of an earlier Saxon original which was granted about 1070 to Lewes Priory. It was rebuilt in the 14th century and the tower was rebuilt after a fire in 1683.

But standard of construction wasn't always guaranteed and it collapsed in 1785, damaging much of the church in the process. It was one James Wyatt who rebuilt nearly all of the building in 1789, and it was restored in 1874.

Links with earlier centuries of worship are not entirely lost. At the foot of the chancel steps is a grave-slab of Sussex iron to a lady called Anne Barcley, who died in 1570. It serves as a reminder of East Grinstead's iron past.

East Grinstead

Sackville College at East Grinstead looks like a house for country gentry that has strayed into the town.

Today 17 old people live in the historic surroundings of this Jacobean-style manor house in what must be the most distinguished old folk's home in the county.

They owe their good fortune to the Second Earl of Dorset, Robert Sackville. He died in 1609 but not before he had the idea for a halfway house for his own convenience when travelling between his Sussex estates and London — combined with a building that would also serve to help the citizens of East Grinstead.

His intention was to build a college or hospital and "to bestow on the building thereof the sum of £1,000 or such a sum as shall be necessary, and to endow the same with a rent charge of £330 a year out of my lands towards the relief of one and 30 unmarried persons, 21 men and 10 women . . ."

But what Robert Sackville hadn't expected was that he would die before the building could be completed in 1619. The surprise was that his son Richard honoured his father's wishes. Far from philanthropy, he was a renowned spendthrift, always in debt from his wild extravagances and a spender of money on fine clothes, gaming and women rather than the welfare of ordinary people.

But the expected shortcomings were to manifest themselves in his brother and successors. For 60 years the college suffered while they shirked their responsibilities at East Grinstead. Income from the endowment was not coming in and during the Civil War it is said that, in spite of a charter from Charles I, five of the home's residents died of starvation.

Yet the bad times passed and today the college survives with only slight alterations. The residents are generally always drawn from East Grinstead but if there are no suitable candidates then people from throughout Sussex are considered.

Until not so long ago a bell tolled the day of the month, the month of the year and each 24 hours. The residents were known as brethren and wore cassocks, while the sisters had capes and bonnets embroidered with the Sackville arms.

ETCHINGHAM CHURCH BUILT 1360 1970.

Etchingham

The essence of the beautiful village of Etchingham, on the west side of the Rother and inland from Hastings, lies in its exquisite church.

It was built around 1363 by Sir William de Echyngham in the decorated style and has some of the most delicate and enchanting flowing tracery found on any church windows in Sussex.

That's not all it has which makes it unique in the county. For here can be found the oldest dated brass in Sussex, an effigy of Sir William in armour and two inscriptions recording in Latin his building of the church and in Norman-Latin his death in 1388.

The church also has what some have claimed is the oldest copper weather vane in England and another brass with a triple canopy dedicated to Sir William's son.

Among its other treasures are 18 carved oak stalls with misereres of the 14th century and outside the traditional yew tree, together with a stone cross unveiled by author Rudyard Kipling in memory of men of Etchingham who died in World War I.

Falmer

No one could pretend that Falmer has either the prettiest pond or the prettiest church in Sussex. But put them both together in a blending of nature and man and you have as pretty a complementary picture as you're likely to find.

The church looks older than its actual years. That is hardly surprising since when it was rebuilt in 1815 the architects of the day chose an imitation Norman style to give it a square robust outline.

But the Christian church wasn't the first visitor to Falmer. The earliest inhabitants were the nomadic tribes who grazed their sheep on the nearby downland and who left three bronze armlets here to be discovered thousands of years later.

They came to be called Brighton loops because of their distinctive form, and today these remains of the earliest Falmer residents are housed in Brighton's municipal museum.

The village came nearer in administration to Brighton in 1928 when Falmer, Patcham, West Blatchington, Ovingdean and Rottingdean were all swallowed up in a joint operation designed to preserve Downland and to safeguard water collecting areas.

But the concrete spread of Sussex University, just across the main Brighton-Lewes Road, and the traffic carried by the road itself have not been easy for the village to accommodate.

Felpham

It was at Felpham that William Blake wrote "Heaven opens on all sides her golden gates."

It was here too that he illustrated his prophetic book Jerusalem and began his Milton. And it was here, at Felpham, that Blake had the semi-traumatic experience when he ejected a soldier from his garden only to have him bring a charge of malicious treason against Blake at Chichester. That was when Blake and Felpham parted company.

But Felpham goes back much further. Its community beginning is rumoured to have come with Saxon pirates who camped here during the early days of their invasion. In AD 889 it was mentioned in the will of Alfred the Great, who left it to Osferth, his kinsman.

The Crown again held Felpham in 953 when it was granted by Alfred's grandson, King Ethelred, the friend of St. Dunstan, to his mother Algivra — widow of Edward the Elder.

Around 888 a famous abbey was founded at Felpham by the nuns of Shaftesbury and some historians say that nuns from there built a church in the village during the religious fervour of the 11th century.

During the Reformation all stone altars were removed and the high altar top was taken away and buried. Years later it was found and taken back to the church, where it can still be seen.

Findon

In a valley north of Worthing lies the village of Findon, which was, perhaps, once the sort of wind-sheltered place from which ancient man descended when he climbed down from the roof of Sussex at nearby Cissbury Ring, momentarily leaving behind his Iron Age fort with its flint mines and burial places.

Certainly it is today a village of the sort that gives Sussex its flavour and its charm.

At the heart of Findon is its church, a transitional Norman building that bears evidence to alterations and modifications by many builders through the centuries.

In the 13th century the chancel and chapel were added and in 1867 more extensive restorations were carried out.

Inside are roof beams that probably date back to the 15th century, while on a gable high above the pulpit is an old sanctus bell. The chapel has a 13-century screen, which is reputed to be one of the oldest in Sussex and which, like the sanctus bell, is a rare feature.

To anyone tired of the coastal strip from Worthing to Littlehampton, no better rural ride could be recommended than to a place with the sense of history and the air of relaxation of Findon.

Fishbourne

Fishbourne is a small village west of Chichester. Now a Roman palace which was as big as that of Nero's in Rome has literally emerged from the earth.

It was discovered after centuries of lying submerged beneath the ground by an agricultural worker who in 1960 was working on the straightforward job of digging a drainage trench across a Fishbourne field.

But instead of a resting place for pipes his spade uncovered a historical treasure trove that was once the home of Claudius Cogidubnus, a Briton friendly to the Romans, who provided him with his stupendous palace to help them with their occupation.

Since that fateful drainage trench dig in 1960 the remains have become famous throughout the world for their unique mosaic floors, for the only excavated Roman garden in Britain, for the historical insight into trade and commerce which then used to be conducted in a harbour that stretched right up to the palace door — and perhaps, too, for the splendid modern pavilion that now houses the archaeological wonders left behind after fire burned down this wonderful building so long ago.

Fishbourne must be almost as heavily impregnated now with the atmosphere of Roman Britain as it was in the days when the Second Legion began to herd the brave natives of this island back into retreat and defeat in the West Country.

In Fishbourne and Bignor, where there are the remains of another impressive Roman villa, the footsteps of the conquerors who colonised these islands centuries ago ring down the ages.

Fittleworth

The old mill house at Fittleworth could almost have been built with artists in mind.

Today they come in their scores to record on canvas the pastoral beauties of this building which lends fame to this small village lying between Petworth and Pulborough in West Sussex.

The mill is quiet now. It long ago ceased to earn its living in the original way for which it was intended. The loudest noise hereabouts is the green water of the Rother swirling through its sluices on its way through green Sussex pastures to join the Arun.

Yet its matured walls have echoed to busier days of industry. Between the 13th and 19th centuries the mill was owned by the Bishops of Chichester.

They it was who gained royalties from its earnings and a bonus of golden corn after it had been processed through the everturning wheels.

Not that an exorbitant rent was charged. In 1873, shortly before it was sold, yearly rent for the mill was a mere £6!

Fletching

Fletching is more than a pretty village in East Sussex. It is a place of historical importance to the English tradition of democracy.

It was here in 1264 that Simon de Montfort stayed with his army the night before the Battle of Lewes which took place on the South Downs about eight miles south.

Their roof for the night was the original Fletching Church and legend has it that the knights who died the next day in battle were brought back here and laid to rest under the nave in full armour.

Centuries later there came another man who didn't so much make history but who wrote about it. He was Edward Gibbon, who wrote The Decline and Fall of the Roman Empire in the nearby mansion that is Sheffield Park. It took him from 1766 until 1788. Now he lies buried in a vault at the church.

It is the church which is the focal point of the few timbered streets which make up Fletching. The present building was built around 1340 and boasts a spire of 99ft. In the north aisle is a small 15th century brass to Peter Denot, a local glover who took part in Jack Cade's revolt.

In the Domesday Book they have Fletching as Flescinge and Sheffield as Siffelle, which shows what time can do to a name. But whatever the name some of England's opponents at the Battle of Agincourt had reason to be aware of this particular part of Sussex.

Forest Row

Forest Row is a Sussex village that had its heritage destroyed rather than created by man.

In Saxon times Ashdown Forest was the domain of wolves, wild boars and stags. Going back still further, remains of crocodile and megalosauri have been found.

But for hundreds of years following the Normans, Ashdown Forest was a great hunting ground and the names of places like Friars Gate and Chelwood Gate still show where the kings of England were wont to enter its green domains.

The forest as it is today stems from the year 1693 when, following a Royal Commission, 6,400 acres were set aside in perpetuity for use and enjoyment of Commoners.

But it was the iron industry that turned this part of Sussex into the Black Country of England and saw the ruination of the medieval forest.

It was to the Roman Catholic church in Forest Row that the late President Kennedy came to worship when he stayed with former Premier Macmillan at nearby Birch Grove.

In the village also are the remains of Brambletye, once a splendid mansion house. The original building was recorded in the Domesday survey compiled by the Normans in 1086 and had a history which could be traced back to Saxon times.

Eventually it came into possession of the Compton family who built a new mansion in the 17th century.

Fulking

Across the South Downs from Brighton and Hove, sheltered in the lee of those verdant hills, lies the Downland village of Fulking.

It is, in reality, a collection of some delightful cottages and, of course, the public house for which so many know it — the historic Shepherd and Dog. In bygone years it was a centre of the sheep farming for which the area was renowned. Many a shepherd and many a dog stopped off at the pub after a day, or perhaps a night, tending the flocks of Southdown rams and ewes that in their time brought such prosperity to Sussex.

Geographically and socially Fulking is an integral part of the village network surrounding it. Crowning the whole area is Devil's Dyke itself.

Fulking

It may not be very far in actual miles. But timewise Fulking couldn't be further away from the busy bustle of the South Coast.

This pretty village lies barely eight miles north-west of Brighton. But it represents an atmosphere and sense of the past that has long since vanished from much of the Downs.

Fulking is still remembered for what made the South Downs famous — and that is sheep. The view past the aptly named Shepherd and Dog pub is one that in its days was a common site to generations of sheep farmers who grazed their Southdown flocks on the springy young turf.

The pleasure of Fulking is that it hopefully will never be, and certainly never has been, more than a village sheltering under a lee of the Downs.

It lies between Poynings and Edburton, a merciful byway on the path of history. The village provided some sanctuary during the time of the Black Death. What was then the manor house, built by the Baron de Falke in the 12th century, became a refuge for those who managed to escape from London and its contagion.

Canadians were billeted in Fulking during World War II and wrote to the village after their return thanking the people for their kindness and remarking on the ghost of a white-haired old lady some of them were supposed to have seen carrying a Bible.

Writer John Ruskin apparently wasn't so troubled. He is credited with having started a scheme for improving the water supplies of the hamlet by making Fulking's well-known Downland stream drive a hydraulic ram.

Glyndebourne

If there's one name which brings music to the ears of English opera lovers it is that of Glyndebourne and the world famous festival which attracts thousands each summer season.

But there is more than just an opera festival. There is also the beautiful village of Glynde itself, lying peacefully on a steep hill overlooked by the eastern slopes of the towering Mount Caburn.

You can get from Lewes to Glynde by footpath. John Ellman is bound to have used that very path in the years of his mortal span from 1753 to 1832. He was the man who perfected the breeding of Southdown sheep, for which Sussex is famous. He farmed at Glynde and is buried in the churchyard.

Centrepiece of the village is Glynde Place, an early Elizabethan house built of flint and Caen stone enclosing a churchyard.

This delightful residence was designed in 1569 for William Morley, one of a family of iron-masters, who lived at Glynde from the reign of Edward IV right up until 1679.

Later it passed to the Trevor family who carried out substantial alterations and remodelled the hall in Georgian style.

Handcross

Nymans Gardens is south of Crawley and just off the Brighton road at Handcross.

It has just about every attraction such a garden could offer, even down to its association with the Royal Family through Lord Snowdon.

The 30-acre gardens were made over to the national Trust in 1954 under the will of Lt. Col. L.C.R. Messel, father of the Countess of Rosse, mother of the former Anthony Armstrong-Jones, and naturally, as such, Princess Margaret's mother-in-law.

Up until 1970 Nymans was attracting something like a yearly 17,000 people. Then Percy Thrower did a programme on the gardens and, as a direct result, by 1971 the attendance had nearly doubled to 34,000.

What in fact he had done was to highlight one of the most unusual English gardens in Sussex. For the secret of Nymans is its sheer intimacy. The grounds are laid out in a series of little gardens, each with its special character and each a perfect compartment of nature reflecting a particular type of flower, shrub or tree.

And while nature is directed, it is not tamed as the romantic ruins of a house destroyed by fire and now delightfully being reclaimed by nature prove. On the ruins of the great hall a Goliath Magnolia chases a double yellow Banksian Rose in a race to the topmost gable.

As for the garden itself it's easy enough to state that it has six sections but it would be a job of catalogue proportions to list the wealth of fauna to be found within them. They break down into a heather garden, the wall garden, made out of an old orchard and with centre paths crossing at an Italian garden, the top garden, the reserve garden and the pinetum, with its huge conifers.

Hardham Priory

William Pricklow was the last canon of Hardham Priory. But his coat of arms hints that he may have enjoyed a good time. It seems to show barrels of beer — heraldic, adorned, but none the less barrels of beer.

The historic coat of arms forms another link with its long past. The priory was founded in 1248 by William Dautrey, grandson of William of Hardham, whose ancestors came to England with William the Conqueror.

The priory was for the Black Canons of St. Augustine and it came endowed with suitable land. But even boozy Canon Pricklow couldn't halt the Dissolution, or at least what followed here shortly afterwards.

It seems Hardham Priory escaped Henry VIII's assault against monasteries but suffered shortly afterwards.

In the interval canons gave an annuity to Thomas Cromwell— Henry's Dissolution draughtsman — for three years and Cromwell himself apparently staved off the fateful day with "prudent counsel and charitable words."

It wasn't enough though. In 1534 the priory closed and was dissolved by agreement between the prior and Sir William Goring, who was then the patron.

Today just the chapter house still stands as a picturesque ruin, which is open to the public by arrangement.

Hastings

Old Hastings Fishermen's Church is now a fishermen's museum. Its chief exhibit is a boat called The Enterprise which was the last of the Hastings luggers built for sail only, a fitting focal point for a salty exhibition.

It was back in 1853 that an application was made for the building of a chapel of ease or church under a 75 year lease at a £ yearly rental.

What arose was the fishermen's church of St. Nicholas, built on unconsecrated ground won from the sea and occupied by the corporation under an Elizabethan charter of 1588.

The war caught up with St. Nicholas's in 1939. It was closed down, used as an army store and eventually war damaged.

Time took its toll too. Floors and wall panellings had rotted and eventually the Old Hastings Preservation Society suggested that the church should become a museum, a suggestion approved by the council in 1955. The building's interior was gutted, leaving only the font, a small gallery and a bell cast in the Whitechapel foundry in 1853.

But from the old arose the new carried in on board the Enterprise and all her nautical atmosphere.

Hastings

Dickens Cottage in Hastings Old Town, with its oak beams and old world charm, looks exactly the sort of place Dickens would have chosen for Tiny Tim to spend Christmas.

The only missing link: Dickens Cottage never received a visit from Charles Dickens.

The author came to Hastings, that much is for sure. It is known he visited the town to pay his last respects to his dying sister who lived in a house called The Briars.

It is also known he came in 1861 to give some readings, but there's nothing on record about a visit to the cottage.

Doubtless Dickens would have loved to pop in; even though he didn't the name is not mere fancy.

The title goes back to the days when Lady Henry Dickens used to visit the cottage. She was the wife of Henry Dickens, the novelist's son — hence the link.

The connection has been enthusiastically maintained by Miss Valette who is a firm friend of Cedric Dickens, another of the novelist's descendants.

Like all the male line members of the family his initials are the same as those of his famous forebear.

Historically the house pre-dates Charles Dickens, Miss Valette claims it incorporates the oldest wall in Hastings, part of an earlier building.

She estimates its age as 400 years and has lived in the house for over 40 years. Time enough to become attached to a home — especially when you've had to fight for it.

That was during World War II when the local authority condemned the property. She campaigned for its preservation — and won.

Preservation was followed by a detailed restoration.

Hastings

Hastings is probably of Saxon origin, as the "ing" at the end of its name indicates.

The name comes from a tribe, the Haestingas, who settled here around the 8th century and who in turn derived their name from Haesta of Haesten, possibly one of the Jutish invaders who overran Kent in the 5th century.

By Saxon times Hastings had become a place of some importance and King Athelstan set up a royal mint in the town in 928.

But obviously it was the Battle of Hastings and the setting up by William of his headquarters on West Hill, before going on to make his principal port here, that has made Hastings a name around the world.

What's left of the atmosphere of that historic past resides today in the town's eastern section known as Old Hastings, and of which this house known as the Pulpit Gate at the bottom of Old Saint's Street still serves as a reminder.

It's from the beach off Old Hastings that the remaining fishing fleets put to sea in their bluff-bowed trawlers, looked down upon by the remains of the castle that separates the modern town from the old.

Further along the West Hill, and overlooking the narrow valley into which the Old Town lies, is the entrance to St. Clement's Caves, a series of caverns covering about three underground acres.

Haywards Heath

History has a habit of repeating itself, they say — but not always in the ways that merit the imitation. Architecturally to be once gone is soon forgotten. But occasionally the clock is turned back to a more gracious period and it has been at Heaselands House, near Haywards Heath.

It's authentic, down to the Horsham stone slabs of the roof, the weathered tiles and all the stylistic devices that have helped create an elegant building erected with the grandeur of less pressured times.

All that's lacking is a circa 1500 date. Heaselands was rebuilt in an otherwise indistinctive architectural year of 1935, on the site of what was previously a much older and smaller house.

Today it is the home of merchant banker Mr. Ernest G. Kleinwort and lies at the heart of his magnificent 1,500-acre estate.

But at Heaselands it isn't only the house that merits attention. To most people Heaselands are the splendid gardens and woodlands that are opened to the public at highlights of the growing seasons.

All funds are for retired nurses. And it's towards open days that head gardener Thomas Cowan and team work to bring the rhododendron garden and the azalea woodland garden to their prime.

Naturally the ornamental gardens have many more attractions besides, 22 to be precise. There's an aviary for foreign birds, and geese and crane on the duck pond and in Goose Paddock.

Later in the summer the rose garden comes into its own and Stepping Stones Valley bursts forth into greenness. And as the 20 years of his work at Heaselands have gone by, Mr. Cowan and his staff have been busy expanding the gardens — a programme they continue each year.

Haywards Heath

If you want to leave your heart in an English Garden you couldn't do better than at Borde Hill, Haywards Heath.

The gardens, which lie sedately on the Balcombe Road, were planned by Col. Stephenson Clarke, who from 1893 until his death in 1948 worked to make this collection of rare trees and shrubs a botanical delight.

The task was carried on by Sir Ralph Stephenson Clarke, a former MP for East Grinstead, until he died in 1970.

At Borde Hill nature and architecture are complemented. Much of the house dates only from 1912, but it has a west front built in 1598 and two interior stone and wood chimney pieces dating from 1601.

Many of the rare shrubs and trees were raised from seeds collected in China, Burma and Tibet between 1912 and 1930.

That was the great era of plant collecting, which was followed by hybridising in private gardens and an ultimate of the British garden scene.

In this period of expansion Borde Hill outgrew itself. The original garden proved too small and the ever-growing collection spilled over into surrounding park and woodlands until some 350 acres were in use.

Henfield

Henfield lies over the Downs from Brighton with a cricket-green aura that places it firmly in the English village slot. It now forms a minor commuter belt for those with jobs on the busy coastal strip, a country retreat that still exudes a red tile and brick tranquillity of its own.

These days Henfield is famous for one piece of its country, the Trust Woods Mill at adjoining Small Dole, headquarters of the Sussex Naturalists Trust.

It stands in 15 acres of land that includes a lake and the beautiful 18th-century house containing an educational museum that in turn contains a restored water mill.

Outside a nature trail winds its way through the marshland, woodland and pasture that through its flora and fauna brings a flavour of authentic countryside.

Henfield's parish church dates back to the 13th and 14th centuries, boasts some brasses of the 16th and 17th centuries and has a 15th-century tower looking out over a community protected by the South Downs and a belt of greenery.

Herstmonceux

Herstmonceux Castle in East Sussex is surrounded by nothing but far seeing men! In fact probably the most far seeing men in the country.

From the grounds of this historic castle begun in 1440 they look out on stars whose glitter stems from millions of light years away —stars suspended in a vastness of time that makes Herstmonceux seem as contemporary as a plastic bubble house.

They are of course the gentlemen and astronomers of the Royal Greenwich Observatory which commenced transfer to the castle grounds from the smog of London in 1948.

Now Herstmonceux boasts the massive Isaac Newton telescope, one of the biggest in Western Europe, standing 48ft. high on a platform in a massive domed building overlooking the Pevensey marshes that have seen so much history.

It was built by one Sir Roger Fiennes as a stronghold and yet he chose bricks as the building material. Consequently Herstmonceux is one of the oldest brick buildings in England and ironically at the same time can be classed as one of its oldest houses.

It rivals Bodiam in appearance and like Bodiam is enclosed by a moat and set low in a secluded valley. Parts of the castle were altered in the 17th century and in 1708 it was sold to George Naylor, whose only daughter is said to have been starved to death by her governess here.

After various other chapters of ownership it was bought by Col. Claude Lowther and a careful reconstruction of the interior was completed in 1935.

Hickstead

Did Hickstead ever exist before Douglas Bunn and his massed legions of show jumpers?

Strange to think, yes it did and a long time ago — when horses were for the eating and suitably insensitive armoured gallants made war seated upon the dray variety.

Mark you, the name might not have immediately seemed the same. In the 14th century it was known as Hestede or Hecgstede and in the 16th it had come down to Hokstede.

But there it was, nestling snug up to Bolney on what was to become the London to Brighton road. The earliest records are when it was a freehold in the manor of Saddlescombe.

One Mathew de la Cumbe owned Hickstead in the 13th century. He went on to give it to his brother Richard and down it tumbled through the families and years until in the 16th century it was acquired by the Stapleys of Twineham Manor.

There was a William and a son John and in 1608 Hickstead was reported as having 93 acres of land before going on to become the manor house to Twineham manor.

And then of course there was Douglas Bunn, wealthy barrister, horse lover and the man who has turned Hickstead into an equestrian Glyndebourne.

He lives in a 16th century Tudor mansion looking over a fair slice of Sussex and the remains of a castle monastery, the floor plan of which pushes up its religious remains in dry periods.

In their time they had both occupied as fine a position as Mr. Bunn enjoys today, commanding upper river reaches and views along to the Downs.

High Salvington

High Salvington is what its place name declares it to be — perched high on the South Downs 350ft. above sea level and with a panoramic view of more than 70 miles of English coastline.

At this village just inland from the modern Worthing that sprawls along the coast is one of the finest windmills that ever ground corn in Sussex.

It was built in 1745 around a centre post cut from a living oak tree and is one of the oldest specimens of its kind in the country.

It ceased its productive life in 1897 when it was sold on the condition that it would be kept in the same state as when the miller ground his last sack of corn there.

But a promise made all those years ago when the windmill was the only development on the top of High Salvington Hill, wasn't enough to preserve it from the inroads of time.

Ravages of weather and lack of attention at one time reduced the mill to a sad remnant of its original self, with two of its four sweeps having disappeared and wooden slats hanging forlornly from the main bodywork.

But it takes more than mere neglect to erase the history of so robust a landmark. The mill still stands proud today, benefitting from the attention of admirers and others.

Hooe

It's the shepherds of the Pevensey Marshes on the one hand and the Abbot of Battle on the other that we have to thank for the Lamb Inn, which dates back to at least 1520 at Hooe.

It all started around the windswept Pevensey area that the Romans called Anderida and which nowadays retreats before the expansion of Bexhill.

Then as now cruel biting winds blew in from the sea during winter months to make life tougher than most modern men can comprehend for those guarding the flocks of Sussex sheep.

So with a gesture of rare enlightenment a long-ago abbot of Battle is reputed to have given permission for an inn to be built at Hooe on the marsh as a halfway house between grazing pasture and shepherds' homes.

A charter granted special dispensation to any shepherd with a sick animal to bring it in before the huge inglenook fireplace to benefit from a literal spell of the warmth of human kindness.

The few shepherds today on the marshes still find the fire kept burning as brightly as ever down the years. By tradition a special blaze of logs is kept stoked up day and night from January to April for the lambing season.

This picturesque village is not without the traditions of history itself. The gentle stream of the Ashburn passes through its territory and the church is dedicated to St. Oswald, King of Northumbria.

Houghton Bridge

The picturesque bridge at Houghton spans more than the River Arun. It also spans the centuries.

A bridge has helped travellers on their way in this quiet corner of Sussex near Amberley for 600 years. There's no specific record but it's safe to say that King Charles II was especially grateful. But then he was fleeing Cromwell's chasing roundheads after the Battle of Worcester.

History has him crossing into Sussex from Hampshire and heading for Arundel before turning down Houghton Hill and crossing the Arun by Houghton Bridge.

And then history has him sensibly stopping for a drink! It was at Houghton's historic George and Dragon Inn in 1651 and a plaque remembering that the monarch "stopped to take ale" records the event to this day.

Suitably refreshed, the king then went on to Bramber and eventually Southwick before finally sailing with Capt. Tattersall to Fecamp in France.

It wasn't the only event of note in Houghton. Three hundred and fifty years before King Charles, the Earl of Arundel apologised to the Bishop of Chichester here after a row.

It had arisen when the earl's dogs had wandered in the bishop's forest, no less, and after the earl had been brought to his knees by the bishop resorting to the spiritual blackmail of excommunication.

The earl found he couldn't get in church, his people were refused the sacrament and even burial rights. In 1292 at Houghton he apologised.

The present bridge over the Arun is of five-arch mock Tudor construction and looks like something straight from France and Brittany. It was built in 1875 to replace a bridge built in 1440 by Bishop Party.

Hurstpierpoint

Hurstpierpoint is Sunday summer escape for those who want refuge from Brighton and the coastal strip.

It lies over the Downs near its neighbour Hassocks, as yet unspoiled by the growing suburban commuter belt of those who work by day in the offices and factories of the Five Towns.

Needless to say there were earlier residents. You can still see a few Georgian houses to prove it and then there's the Gothic revival church built in 1845 by Sir Charles Barry, with its lofty spire pointing straight and true into the Sussex sky.

Step inside and there's a 14th century altar tomb with a mutilated effigy of a knight, all surrounded by a 16th century iron railing with candle prickets. Here too are 16th century German or Flemish roundels of glass and near the west door outside there are a great number of time-worn medieval tiles.

The village came by its name through the De Pierpoints in the 12th century. And in Elizabethan times it came into another slice of history — the stately brick mansion of Danny, built below the promontory of Wolstonbury Hill by George Goring, who later became Lord Goring of Hurstpierpoint.

But to many who no longer live in the county, Hurstpierpoint is still a vivid memory. They are the boys who through the generations have been pupils at the college which bears the name of the village.

SHOREHAM GRAMMAR SCHOOL, KINGSTON — Gerald Lip

Kingston

Shoreham Grammar School, in the rural parish of Kingston, is one of those places that combines both old and new.

The building itself is Tudor, with oak panelling inside, flint walled exterior and generally of the gracious proportions of that outstanding period of English architecture.

The flavour of youth comes from the 187 pupils who have attended the school since it moved there in 1968.

For them history is literally in the classroom and on the doorstep.

Kingston boasts a church steeped in antiquity. It was first built in early Norman times and was largely rebuilt in the 13th century.

Called St. Julian's, it was mentioned in the Domesday Book, when the parish of Kingston was called Chingestune.

When it was rebuilt the central tower was raised, and its groined vaults carried on clustered shafts with carved capitals.

The nave has a Jacobean pulpit and reading desk, the chancel a restored 15th century screen and a 15th century canopied tomb that served as an Easter sepulchre.

When the pupils of the grammar school have classes in ecclesiastical architecture Kingston and St. Julian's provide the subject.

LANCING SCHOOL AND CHAPEL — Gerald Lip 1969.

Lancing

Lancing Chapel is the perfect blend between beauty and size.

As the most famous landmark of that famous boys' public school it looms on the Sussex Downs facing the sea. The foundation stone was laid in 1868.

It is designed on the same scale as the naves of Westminster Abbey and York Minster and even though its vintage is of relatively recent date it has been built in the tradition of medieval abbeys.

No machinery has been used and the stone was quarried at Scaynes Hill by the members of one family and cut and laid by hand.

The College has never employed a contractor for the chapel but has directly employed craftsmen with a system of apprenticeship set up which has meant that many masons have learnt their skills at Lancing.

That is why many consider the building to be one of the finest Gothic structures built in England since the close of the Middle Ages.

Today, and since the end of the war, there has existed a body called the Society of Friends of Lancing Chapel. Their aim is to collect and organise funds.

The building reflects the inspiration of the school's famous founder Nathaniel Woodard.

When the foundation stone was laid over a century ago the great church was regarded as "Woodard's Folly" because at the time there was no money to guarantee its completion.

Today it stands a testimony to his vision as a great educationist and Christian.

Lewes

Lewes Castle stands on a ridge where it was designed to defend the narrow gap by which the Ouse passes the town. It was built soon after the Conquest by William de Warenne, the first Earl of Surrey, and it fits in exactly with the early Norman style of motte and bailey except that the historians tell us it is unique in having two separate mottes, or mounds.

But there's nothing gaunt and stark about the remains of Lewes Castle, which have delighted visitors over the years.

It lies just off the High Street, an artery of paralysis instead of life to the town, and faces the 16th century Barbican House, headquarters of the Sussex Archaeological Society who in turn guard the castle for posterity.

The bailey was entered by a Norman gatehouse and the south and east sides still remain protected by the splendid Barbican or outergatehouse. It was built in the 14th century and is the finest remaining castle feature.

This is a massive three-storey building with twin circular towers on the outside and with the stoutest defence work in the form of knapped and squared flintwork and the cruciform arrow-loops.

The castle in fact dates back to the very beginnings of the importance of Lewes as a county town. William de Warenne was one of William the Conqueror's most powerful followers. His wife founded the splendid priory of St. Pancras south of the town at Southover.

And with soldiers to guard the settlement from castle battlements Lewes flourished as a river and port market town to have its own guild of merchants established before 1147.

So consequently Lewes and its castle came to experience a rich slice of history. The De Warennes were staunch royalists and sided with Henry III in his struggle against rebels led by Simon de Montfort at the famous Battle of Lewes itself.

The harassed king took refuge in the priory in 1264 while his son, later Edward I, made his headquarters in the castle.

Lindfield

When Sir David Hunt says the English climate is the world's best and then chooses to live in a village like Lindfield you can be sure there's nothing rash about the decision.

He settled at Old Place a year ago after his world-trotting career as a diplomat had taken him to every corner of the globe. And he's loved every minute of it since.

Sir David was personal secretary at No. 10 to both Sir Winston Churchill and Mr. Attlee when they were prime ministers. During the war he served in the Middle East and North Africa, was mentioned in despatches three times, won the U.S. Bronze Star to boot, finishing up with the rank of colonel.

Among his many diplomatic jobs were postings to Lahore as UK Commissioner, Uganda, Cyprus, and eventually as the British ambassador in Brazil.

It was in Uganda as High Commissioner that he first met the famed Colonel Amin — when the colonel was an ordinary soldier receiving his first stripe and ominously as heavyweight boxing champion of East Africa.

Amin was responsible for helping to mop up African terrorists. He was very rough, says Sir David with diplomatic recollection.

Now he travels from Lindfield to London in a new capacity as chairman of the governors of the Commonwealth Institute, an organisation whose aim is to spread knowledge of the Commonwealth among British people, especially the young.

But it's a relatively settled life after years as a diplomatic nomad and he has found Old Place better than any embassy. The house was built in the 16th century and was extensively restored and expanded in 1881 by stained glass artist William Kemp.

His works abound throughout the house, each one with his distinctive wheatsheaf motif.

Sir David is more than thankful to Mr. Kemp. He says the Victorian workers he brought in were so much better than the Elizabethan ones who originally built the property.

Lindfield

Lindfield is a picture-postcard village. It lies in the rolling Sussex countryside near Haywards Heath and is the classic English concept of a village, with its cluster of houses grouped round the mother church.

There's the pond, a Tudor house near the church and a common which for centuries was the scene of the annual sheep fair when Sussex was a major sheep-rearing county.

The church itself has been much restored but the tower and north and south aisles are of genuine 13th century manufacture.

Rood-stairs were discovered in the south transept in 1936 — just a year before one of the oldest brasses taken from the church at some unknown time found its way back there.

In the porch is a priest's room — or parvis as some prefer to call it — which now holds a small museum of local history.

But as for Lindfield itself, the village is a living museum showcase of the beauty that is Sussex.

Litlington

Litlington is a rural symphony composed of green countryside, beautiful views of Cuckmere Haven, the flint cottages of a true Downland village and the ever restful sight of aged yet ageless buildings like Church Farm.

It all nestles on a shelf in the verdant Downs near Alfriston, with the Cuckmere River meandering its lazy way through the village on to the sea.

Litlington is in all ways a place with prospects. From here one can see the Downs "cathedral" of Alfriston Church, and nearby is the nature reserve land at Lullington Heath.

The parish church dates back to the 12th and 14th centuries and it is more than possible that the next door Church Farm was once the priest's house.

Lullington Church

Intimate is one description which Lullington Church certainly deserves. It qualifies for the adjective by being the smallest listed in the country still in use.

A total of 22 people can be accommodated in this small sanctuary of Christian worship, lying within a shady circle of elms near Alfriston. It is a perfect example of improvisation in the face of an act of God that was supposed to have destroyed the original church by fire.

All that was spared was part of the chancel. So the villagers decided that a little church was better than no church at all and they walled it up to form the 16 sq. ft. building that exists to this day.

It was in 1966 that pupils of an Eastbourne secondary school proved once and for all that Lullington Church is an existing remnant of a formerly larger building.

Under the supervision of the Sussex Archaeological Society, they dug down to find an outline of a nave and also to give greater strength to the speculation that building on the site dates back to the 12th century.

The fabric of the mini-church that remains dates back to the 13th century. The weather-boarded belfry was erected about 1806. And through a wall thought to be part of the original building is a small window through which it is believed lepers, who were only allowed outside, stood to receive the Sacrament.

There are no lepers now for the services held here once every month during the summer. But then there are no Lullington villagers, either, because the hamlet no longer exists.

It certainly flourished in a quiet way during the Middle Ages and at that time drew some community existence from a now overgrown route which crossed the River Cuckmere. But possibly around the 17th century Alfriston grew in size and local importance to attract away the last of the Lullington villagers.

Midhurst

Cowdray Park at Midhurst is the home today of Lord Cowdray, one of the richest men in England. It lies surrounded by a vast estate of forestry acres and it houses also the noble ruins of the great Tudor building that was once the manor house.

It has also seen the postwar revival of polo, with the Duke of Edinburgh attracting fresh publicity and crowds to an ancient sport.

The present Cowdray House is a Victorian building one mile east of the ruins. It is a place of turrets, gables and tile-hanging, built in a style which easily manages to avoid the architectural pomposity that sometimes makes work of the period overbearing.

The original Cowdray House was destroyed by fire in 1793, on the fateful night of September 24.

The ruins of the original house where it all was reputed to have happened still provide the historical focus at Cowdray. It took 60 years to build under three owners and was begun by Sir David Owen, Owen Glendower's son, who inherited Cowdray in 1492.

As for polo at Cowdray it was brought here when the first Lord Cowdray came to the estate in 1908.

Midhurst

The name Midhurst is Saxon and means "middle wood." It was in the reign of Henry I (1100-35) that Midhurst was first heard of.

In those days the manor was part of the "honour" of Arundel then held by the King. It was granted to Savaric Fitzcane, from whom it passed to Franco de Bohun, the first of a family to hold it until 1499.

From an early date Midhurst was a market centre and in the 16th century the manor passed to the Viscounts Montagu, under whose influence the town became a centre of Roman Catholicism in the succeeding century.

From 1301 until 1832 the town had the honour to send two MPs to parliament but in 1883 it was disfranchised completely — even though in 1761 it had been represented by General Sir John Burgoyne and Sir William Hamilton, husband of Nelson's Emma.

If you are entering from Petworth and Haslemere watch out for the grammar school, founded in 1672 by Gilbert Hannam, a Midhurst coverlet maker. Among the school's most famous pupils have been Sir Charles Lyell, the geologist, and the historian and novelist H. G. Wells.

Close by is the Angel Hotel, said to have been given its name by a band of pilgrim fathers en route to Southampton in the early 1600's. Pass down Knockhundred Row and you come to the centre of the old town. Here is the famous Spread Eagle Hotel, which was first built in the 15th century and then extended in the 17th; the brick and timber Market Hall, built in 1552, and the old town hall near which can still be seen the town stocks and pillory.

Eastwards of Market Square and overlooking the Rother is St. Anne's Hill. This is a lofty mound on top of which are the restored foundations of a castle or fortified manor house of the de Bohuns abandoned by them for Cowdray around the year 1280 and partly dismantled by Antony Bek, Bishop of Durham from 1283 to 1311.

Midhurst

What's left of Cowdray Castle today are the castle ruins in the vast grounds of Cowdray Park, a mile away from the Victorian house near Midhurst where the present Lord Cowdray lives.

Fate took a wrong turn from the time of Henry VIII when Sir Anthony Browne is supposed to have made a gift of Battle Abbey to the then Cowdray occupant.

He turned out the monks and made the abbey into his home.

But not surprisingly for the times, one of the more militant among them had the foresight to lay a curse. The last departing monk warned his oppressor that his line would perish by fire and water.

The water part came true when the first Lord Montagu died in the Rhine accident, and his nephews were drowned. The fire part of the prophecy became a reality in September, 1793, when the castle itself was destroyed by fire.

It needn't necessarily have been. Legend has it that the blaze took hold when workmen employed in the south wing carelessly left a fire burning. The fire was discovered, but not the key to a shed housing the primitive fire engine, and so Cowdray Castle became the ruin it is today.

The loss of the Tudor building to archaeology was enormous. It was begun by Sir David Owen, Owen Glendower's son, who inherited it in 1492. He died in 1535, and lived at Cowdray until his death.

The estate had previously been bought in 1529 by Sir William Fitzherbert and permission to crenellate was granted in 1533.

Fitzherbert was a favourite of the King's and was made Earl of Southampton in 1537 and Lord Keeper of the Privy Seal in 1539.

He added the gatehouse and hexagonal tower and built the hall porch, before dying in 1542 and leaving Cowdray to Sir Anthony.

Certainly, one way or another, they all contrived to have Cowdray largely finished when Queen Elizabeth came visiting. On her stay she is credited with having shot a deer and spent such a good time in Sussex that it drew from her "gentle applause."

Newhaven

Newhaven is the gateway to Sussex and to England.

Through this booming port in summer pass countless thousands of motorised holidaymakers from the Continent driving off the cross-Channel car ferries to make way for English motorists heading the other way.

But through is the operative word. Rarely do they stop to savour the history of a town with an individual past all of its own.

It was well in advance of his contemporary Frenchmen in their cars that Louis Philippe escaped to England via Newhaven in 1848. He stayed overnight at the Bridge Hotel.

Newhaven was originally known as Meeching and first achieved significance in Tudor times.

Then the Ouse, which had previously entered the Channel through Seaford, broke through the shingle bank retaining it and reached the sea under Castle Hill.

But it was in 1566 that the name New Haven was first used and by the 17th century Sussex foundries were exporting their ironware goods through the port.

Newhaven also managed to build up a reputation for itself in the field of ship-building.

The parish church has an unusual Norman tower and apse with a chancel arranged underneath it.

But before that was ever erected for the religious good of the town's inhabitants, earlier people had occupied Castle Hill itself.

Evidence has been found that during the Bronze and Iron ages it was occupied as a fort.

Ovingdean

Ovingdean lies in a fold of the green Downs, just inland from the coastal road and a mere stone's throw from the bustling provincial centre that is Brighton.

Today it's almost as peaceful round its green as when the Saxons came to Ovingdean to build a church. The building is still standing largely unspoiled, dedicated now as then to the Saxon St. Wulstan.

The church has a 12th century nave and chancel, with herring-bone work in flint and the original chancel arch.

Its sturdy tower dates back to about 1200 and the south wall of the nave was then pierced about this time, possibly for an aisle. But this was apparently destroyed in the 14th century — perhaps by a French raid in 1377 — and the arcade blocked up.

After the Saxons came the Normans and the church has many small Norman windows and a blocked up doorway from the same period in the north wall of the nave. Much later by far came the south chapel, which was rebuilt in 1912 on its original 13th century foundations.

Ovingdean is largely centred on the church and Ovingdean Grange, a house of the 16th and early 19th centuries. This restful building was the setting for a now forgotten novel by Harrison Ainsworth telling how Charles II came to Ovingdean after his escape from Worcester.

Peacehaven

Peacehaven was once called Anzac-on-sea — in tribute to Australian and New Zealand troops stationed there during World War 1. But it isn't only in the normal geographical sense that Peacehaven features thus on the maps.

Peacehaven is in the direct path of the prime meridian line, so sharing a geographical position in common with that of Greenwich Observatory.

The obelisk marks the exact point on the cliffs where the line crosses The Promenade.

It is something of a tribute as well to Peacehaven's salty sense of practicability. For when those early residents first raised the cash for their stone tower they also had in mind that it would celebrate the Silver Jubilee of King George V and Queen Mary.

The only snag with that was that the King died before it could be completed. So the obelisk was dedicated to his memory instead.

There's nothing so grand to keep alive the memory of the earliest residents. But then contrary to opinion that nothing goes back to before 1915 and the conception of this garden city by the sea, people were living here long ago — a cool 4,000 years is the guess of some.

Archaeological digs have turned up evidence of habitation for that length of time as well as Stone Age flints at an Arundel Road site and traces of a Saxon burial ground at Friars Avenue.

Romans, too, must have marched across areas of Peacehaven, for which a new town centre and heart is planned by East Sussex County Council. They were garrisoned nearby at Telscombe Cliffs and The Highway at Peacehaven has traces of an original Roman road.

Smugglers came later, of course, as they always did along stretches of Sussex coast almost made to benefit them and hinder customs men.

But Peacehaven did not get under way proper until 1914 when businessman Charles Neville bought 600 acres of land at about £15 an acre from the Cavendish Land Co.

Pett

You can see France from Pett on a clear day. From Chick Hill, in this parish near Winchelsea and up on the Sussex borders with Kent, a view stretches forth that takes in not only the outline of the Continent but also a massive picturesque sweep of the county itself.

From officialdom's point of view Pett is in the Rye division of the county, the hundred of Guestling, the rape and county court district of Hastings and the rural district of Battle. You can add to that also the archdeaconry of Hastings and the diocese of Chichester.

But when all that's said and done Pett has a character all of its own. Once the Royal Military Canal used to terminate here.

But the sea has always had a stronger influence. In many parts of the parish various ancient trees have been dug up which were supposed to have been buried since October in the year of 1250 when waves burst inland and invaded vast areas of country.

And accounts have it that they've been dug up in good condition, too, despite the centuries in an earthy grave of the stiff loam soil on which Pett stands.

But time in this farthest corner of Sussex moves slowly. The parish register of the church of St. Mary and St. Peter dates from 1612, although the present church was rebuilt in 1864.

It is made of stone and in the decorated style. All that probably remains of the original church is an ancient small brass inscription at the base of the chancel arch.

Petworth

The first mention of Petworth was about 791 in a grant made by Eardwulf, king of Northumbria, to St. Peter's at Rome. When Edward the Confessor came to the throne the manor was held by his queen and by 1086 it became the property of Roger de Montgomery, the first Earl of Arundel.

After that the manor was part of the lands given by Henry I to his second wife Adeliza and after long being a seat of the Percy family passed to the Egremonts, who are still at Petworth today.

Petworth to many means Petworth House. The massive baronial mansion dominates the town from behind a wall reputed to be 10 miles long.

In it are a wealth of artistic and cultural treasures. One of the most valuable private art collections in the country has works by William Blake and paintings by Van Dyck and Turner, who painted some of his finest works in the Petworth area.

The first Petworth House was built when licence to "crenellate" — the ancient word for fortify — was given to Henry, Lord Percy, in 1293.

But Petworth House as it is today was built between 1688 and 1696. It is constructed of the same Petworth marble quarried locally from which the Archbishop's chair at Canterbury was hewn.

Pevensey

Pevensey lies in the windswept marshland east of Eastbourne. It was here that William the Conqueror came ashore before he went on to victory at the Battle of Hastings.

But even before William there were the Romans. Pevensey village itself occupies the site of the Roman harbour. And of course it was the Romans, with their romantically named fort, Anderida, who laid the foundations of what the Normans later made into Pevensey Castle.

These first conquerors founded the fort towards the end of the 3rd century and it was one of a great chain built around the Saxon shore. According to the Anglo-Saxon chronicle, it was overwhelmed by Saxon invaders in 491.

It was not until the Normans arrived that the fort came to life again. William granted the Rape of Pevensey to his half-brother Robert, Count of Mortain, who erected an earth and timber castle.

After that it had the stormiest of histories. It was taken by siege in 1088 and again besieged in 1147, when it withstood all attack but was finally taken because of its defenders' hunger. Yet again in 1264-5 it was besieged, this time by Simon de Montfort.

The final assault came after it had been granted to John of Gaunt, Duke of Lancaster, and was besieged by Richard II. By then it was partly ruined already.

In 1925 the ruins were presented by the Duke of Devonshire to the Ministry of Works.

Piddinghoe

In the green sculptured valley of the Ouse, inland from Newhaven and tucked away from the coastal strip, lies the small and beautiful parish of Piddinghoe.

Small is the appropriate word. The village is under 1,000 acres in size — and that includes the inland water that gives its atmosphere the tang of sea and harbour.

Pidd'n'oo it is to the locals and that's doubtless how the parish has been called by those who have been born there down the centuries.

The parish church is that of St. John's. Its register of baptisms goes back to 1540, of marriages to 1555 and burials to 1592.

As for the church itself, it is a flint testimony to the early English and Norman styles of architecture. The nave, with its arcades and the north aisle, are Norman, but the chancel and the chancel arch are of the 13th century.

The tower spire holds three bells and the south aisle and chapels were restored in 1882 for the princely sum of £2,000.

Piddinghoe's charm has naturally not gone unnoticed by previous generations. Prominent to visitors at the village is the trout weathervane on the conical cap of the church tower which was the "begilded dolphin" of Kipling's famous poem "Sussex."

And, with the sea so near, there are the little ships, colourful ketches, clinker-built dinghies, motor boats and all the various craft whose owners have been attracted to the cloistered quiet of so peaceful a stretch of water and land merged together in harmony.

Polegate

Enthusiasm has kept the sails of Polegate Windmill turning. In 1962 it was a sorry, decaying relic of the days when wind supplied the power to turn the grain into flour.

Time had begun to clog up the machinery, some of the wooden structure was rotten and householders in the area were complaining about the eyesore.

But the lists were entered by Eastbourne and District Preservation Society. Their chief ally was the mill's owner, Mr. Albert Ephraim Ovenden, whose father bought the place in 1918.

He agreed to part with the mill for £1,000 to ensure its preservation — and turned down an offer of £2,500 for the land.

The mill was built in 1817 for Joseph Seymour, who came from Pounsley, near Blackboys, and settled in Willingdon about 1800.

He became a farmer of some substance and in 1833 had a watermill built 300 yards to the west of the original windmill. The year 1845 also saw him buy Wannock Watermill and its surrounding six acres.

From then down to the Ovendens the mill passed through a variety of hands. Joseph Seymour left it to his son Joseph Jnr., then it was owned by one Matthias Mockett, who kept the sails turning and the beer flowing in a joint life as landlord of the Red Lion at Willingdon.

When it came down to Ephraim Ovenden in 1918 the mill was on the way into temporary obscurity. The family worked it by wind until 1943 when the fan staging became unsafe. After that and until the end of its working life in 1965 electricity took over.

The mill is 47 feet high with walls more than 2 feet thick at the base.

But the preservationists didn't stop when they had secured the building from time. They turned an old building originally used as an outhouse and store into a mill museum.

Poling

Knights Templars put down their roots at the cosy hamlet of Poling, near Arundel, and built St. John's Priory.

Legend has it that there is an underground crypt where the Knights were buried.

The Knights Templars were an ancient militant Society whose members carried a banner of chivalry. Later the Priory saw another order installed, the Knights of St. John of Jerusalem.

In 1541, at the time of the Dissolution, King Henry VIII handed over the Priory to the College of Arundel.

The Priory then had a succession of private owners, including the Shelleys of poetic fame, before being sold to the Duke of Norfolk in 1828, by which time it had been run down to drab farmhouse status and named Fairplace Farm.

At the beginning of the century Mr. Philip Johnston, a well known authority on Sussex churches, restored the house for his brother, Sir Harry Johnston, a famous explorer of Africa.

Before this restoration ghostly Gregorian chantings accompanied by reedy instruments are rumoured to have been heard in the house over the years.

Poynings

If any one village captures the essence and atmosphere of the South Downs it is surely Poynings.

It lies inland from Brighton, just below the entrance to Devil's Dyke and is sheltered on the east by Newtimber Hill.

The heart of the village is the church, roughly laid out in the shape of a Greek cross. Its beauty is all the more interesting for being original. It is largely unspoiled and as it was when built in late 14th century style with a bequest made by a certain Michael de Poynings, who died in 1396.

The name dates back to the descendants of the Norman lord of the manor, William Fitzrainald, who took the name of Poynings.

They were famous as soldiers and statesmen for 400 years and Michael himself fought at Crecy and Poitiers.

The only thing about Poynings that has not kept pace with its reputation as the perfect Sussex Downland village is its size.

Along with the nearby hamlets of Fulking and Edburton, visitors see a village unaltered since the Sussex shepherds tended their flocks hereabouts in the county's great sheep-rearing days.

Rodmell

Rodmell village is in reality little more than a street nestling in the valley of the River Ouse just inland from Newhaven.

It is made more famous than even its charm and beauty would allow by the residence here up to her sad death in 1941 of the novelist Virginia Woolf.

With her husband, Leonard, who died only recently, she lived in Monk's House, the last in the village street.

The building that housed two such figures of English literature is next door to what is Rodmell's undoubted greatest glory—its restored Norman church.

The nave, chancel and probably the south chapel too are of the early 12th century and Norman windows are distinctive in the chancel, the tower and the baptistry.

Look out too for the palimpsest or double-sided brass hanging on the pier of the chapel. On one side it bears an inscription to John and Agatha Broke (1438) and on the other to John de la Chambre (1673).

And if it's stained glass really brings home the pleasures of a country church to you, there's a circular window in the nave with a group of the Trinity and dating back to the 15th or 16th century.

In the church tower are preserved carved stones of the Norman chancel arch while in the baptistry is a square 12ft. font and an old weathervane constructed of Sussex iron.

Rottingdean

Tallboy Cottage at Rottingdean is now a shop but was once the customs house. Rottingdean had built up something of a reputation as a quiet and sheltered spot outside Brighton where contraband brandy and other smuggled items could be landed without too much trouble.

Smugglers didn't have it all their own way but then neither did customs. 1733 was such an occasion. It was then there was a great fight between the two sides which resulted in the customs men being bound, gagged and left in a barn behind Tallboy Cottage while the smugglers made off with goods that had been impounded.

It was a shortlived victory but one that has down the years constituted a colourful chapter in the history of Rottingdean, Brighton's village by the sea-side.

There were no such irregularities when novelist D. H. Lawrence arrived in 1909. He was a schoolteacher in Croydon, fresh down from industrial Nottingham. He cycled over the Downs to Brighton. He found it stately but wrote to a friend "I am not, so I pushed my way through the wind and here I am at Rottingdean."

Rottingdean's fame has also spread on the sails of the Beacon Hill windmill. It was built before 1800 and moved to the present site by oxen from an original situation further inland.

In 1897 artist William Nicholson drew it and the windmill has since known worldwide fame after the drawing became adopted as the trademark of publishers William Heinemann and Sons.

TALLBOYS, ROTTINGDEAN

Rottingdean has attracted as residents the famous like Rudyard Kipling and the not-so-famous, like Prince Peter Kropotkin. Before the Russian revolution of 1917 the prince was one of many Russians put in prison for revolutionary activities. But he escaped, came to England and set up residence for most of his 40 years in this country at Chesham Street, Kemp Town, and at Rottingdean.

When he left to return to his native land he was presented with a trades council illuminated address which testified to the help he had given the English worker.

Rusper

Up country from the Sussex coastal strip, five miles north-east from Horsham and in the Rape of Bramber, lies the little English village of Rusper. The word English is more than just stating the obvious. Rusper is a rustic gem which makes the very word English mean and stand for what it does. As with all such villages the centre and heart is the church. St. Mary Magdalene is constructed of stone in the Early English style, appropriately enough, and was partially rebuilt in 1855 to conform to the highest standards of Victorian religious demand. It contains a 14th century brass with two half-length figures and an inscription in Norman French — plus another of the 16th century. Take a good look too at the candelabra. They date from 1500 and were discovered in a nearby pond before being restored to something approaching their original condition.

Rye

Gibbet Mill is circa 1930 and its sweeps have never turned.

There was a "genuine" Gibbet Mill all right. But Friday, June 13, 1930, was particularly unlucky. The original building burned down, the cause thought to be an overheated oven.

But Rye without its mill was rather like London without its Tower. So the local council decided that, as a grand gesture to historical continuity and the landscape, the owner should be called upon to provide a replacement.

He did. It cost just over £800, was built of the original brickwork and was nothing but a super facsimile with an empty inside.

Owners of the mill, then as now, were the Webbs, bakers of Rye since 1917, and represented today by third generation baker Mr. Alan Webb. The original mill was operated by Mr. Webb's grandfather who came to the town as a miller and merchant baker.

But the present Mr. Webb has done more than keep the replacement building as a bumper souvenir. Today it turns out real bread, housing the three-man bakery, with offices, on the first floor.

The irony is that the facsimile mill has cost more to maintain than to build in 1930. Partly to blame were the cast iron nails then used in the construction instead of galvanised ones. They simply fell out and the mill, in turn, fell into disrepair.

That led to another colourful chapter for Gibbet Mill, so named because it faces Gibbet Marshes — a favourite medieval execution site.

Mr. Webb cocooned his building, having the mill sheathed in glass plastic in 1968 at a cost of £1,200 and gaining a subsequent £200 grant from East Sussex County Council and himself some world-wide publicity.

So today the dummy mill is a scheduled building.

Rye

Rye is a pot-pourri of cobbled streets, narrow lanes and wooden houses. Once it boasted the sea, too, but that has retreated with the changing shore line.

In the Middle Ages Rye was attached to the confederation of Cinque Ports as an "ancient town." Then it was an important maritime port. Now that trade has been reduced to work which takes place in the harbour of a Rother estuary.

The town stands on a hill overlooking the marshy salt flats that stretch into nearby Kent. Back around 1030 it was part of the manor of Romslie granted by Canute to the Abbey of Fecamp. But two centuries on, Henry III thought it might be used as a bridgehead for a French invasion and took it back in exchange for manors in Gloucestershire.

During the Hundred Years War the French sacked the town in 1339, 1360 and again in 1377 when they completed the job by burning almost everything to the ground.

It was left to Edward III to fortify Rye against the marauders with a huge wall and massive gateways completed some time around 1386. But the town had been drained of its energy and it wasn't until the Huguenot cloth-weavers began to set up their looms in Rye after the massacre of St. Bartholomew's Day in 1572 that fortunes began to turn again.

Queen Elizabeth I, in 1573, confirmed its Royal charter and in the 17th century Rye flourished as never before.

St. Leonards

Marie Lebrock was a famous model. Life was New York, Paris, photographers' studios, magazine covers.

Then she moved into art — fine art of course — and ran a top gallery with her husband in London's St. James's, dealing with wealthy art lovers from all over the world.

Her latest achievement is in Victoria Park, St. Leonards. She is a labourer. She has filled 27 bags with rubbish and loaded six collection skips to overflowing with building rubbish. She has also charmed a menacing patch of dry rot into submission.

The catwalk of her ambition in this particular project is quite simple: to restore James Burton's 1830 Clock House into a seaside family home for the Lebrock family.

At this stage, if you knew the exact measure of what she's taken on, you'd be entitled to gasp. The place had been empty for about two years, except for the visitations of vandals who regard a Grade II Department of the Environment listed building as no different from a local pool hall.

And for the past year she and her fellow labourer, a friend who shares her enthusiasm, have been the sole workforce.

There is naturally a picture frame of perspective. Mrs. Lebrock is only a weekend labourer and still lives at St. James's and still is only a weekend labourer and still lives at St. James's weekdays, commuting to the coast for her work-ins.

The main restoration work has yet to be started on the building's exterior and that will get underway when the historic cash grant problem is sorted out.

Seaford

The Martello tower at Seaford is a splendid example of a chain of structures that were built from there to Folkestone as a defence against invasion during the Napoleonic wars.

They are half-conical blockhouses of which Seaford's is the most westerly. It is a massive monument to history.

There is an odd lurid tale about the Seaford Martello Monster.

This was rumoured to be a creature that some years back played havoc with the nets of fishermen. Whether it was a giant angler fish or a huge skate was never discovered.

But whatever the sea monster was a Martello label guaranteed its ill-repute just that little more fame than it might otherwise have expected.

Like the giant tower itself Seaford has seen many changes in the times and its fortunes.

Once this was a port of some significance, until a great storm in 1579 finally deflected the Ouse from Seaford itself to next-door Newhaven.

After the Norman Conquest it was counted first among members of the Cinque Ports attached to Hastings. And during the reign of Edward III it was frequently attacked by the French.

Shipley

No one loved Shipley windmill more than author Hilaire Belloc. He owned it and lived next to it in a rambling house at this village near Horsham. And every time he returned from a walk across the South Downs, which he loved and wrote about so much, he doffed his hat at this white symbol of the Sussex countryside.

Belloc had time to work up his affection. He lived at Shipley for nearly 50 years and it stayed his home until his death in 1953.

Understandably, he was concerned that after he died this fine 1879 example of a smock mill would suffer the fate of so many less robust specimens of history.

He needn't have worried. Today, Shipley mill is in a better state of preservation than ever. In fact it is to Belloc that we should be grateful for the sight of its four sails still sweeping in the wind when the ancient wheels are set turning.

It was in 1958 that restoration of the mill, at a cost of £4,600, was completed — as a giant-sized memorial to Belloc himself. What the author would have appreciated even more was that the initiative came from a committee of local people who raised a large part of the money themselves to save the oldest working smock windmill in West Sussex.

The restoration is complete down to the last detail. The mill is open to the public on certain weekends in the summer.

Sheffield Park

Sheffield Park is a corner of Sussex where time ticks over at the gentle revolutions of a few centuries ago. There's the Bluebell Railway to take travellers back into the leisurely realm of steam travel. And, as the complete gentleman's country experience, there's the remarkable house of Sheffield Park itself and the 150 acres of perfected gardens that surround it.

Following the death of its former owner, industrialist Mr. Lionel McCardle, the contents were sold at the biggest Sussex auction sale of the century. They fetched over £132,000. The house acquired a new owner in the person of Mr. P. J. Radford, an antique expert.

It is a neo-Gothic building of spires and pinnacles that was for many years the country seat of the Earls of Sheffield.

Here it was that around 200 years ago historian Edward Gibbons wrote part of his great work, Decline and Fall of the Roman Empire.

Today, Sheffield Park is administered by the National Trust and has been since 1954. Under their care the woodland and garden heritage so carefully laid down those years ago has grown to attract thousands of holiday makers each summer.

The most notable feature of the gardens are the five lakes laid out on different levels and surrounded by a world-embracing collection of trees. In the grounds are a host of pine trees alone — Monterey pines, Tasmanian pines, Japanese pines, Swiss pines and onwards.

The gardens are open to the public in summer.

Shoreham

Shoreham is now the generally accepted place where Aella, the Saxon chieftain, made his landing in Britain after the Romans had left. It is the place that in 1346 built 26 ships — greater than the numbers turned out by the shipyards of either London or Dover — for Edward III's invasion of France; where in 1199 King John set foot ashore to assume the crown on the death of Richard I and from where, most famous of all, Charles II escaped in 1651 after his forces had been crushed to defeat at the battle of Worcester.

Tucked away behind the shopping street is one of the most charming and graceful churches in Sussex, that of St. Mary de Haura. It is now only a small part in size of the building it once was, and of the Norman nave only a single bay has survived. The Norman church was completed about 1130. But the centuries have seen many additions and adaptations.

Not far away, in the High Street, is an ancient two-storeyed house called the Marlipins. It was built in the 12th century — probably by the De Braose family — as a storage house for wine and other goods taken as tolls from ships entering the port of Shoreham.

The building has a front chequered in flint and Caen stone which was altered in the 14th century. Today it is a museum of prehistoric remains and local relics that bear testimony to the rich and colourful past of Shoreham.

Slindon

Going to school for 75 boys at Slindon College is a history lesson in itself.

When they file into classrooms in the 83-room house they sit at desks in a building that is one of the finest mansions in Sussex and which was a famous centre of Catholicism.

Slindon House, which accommodates the college, can trace its roots back to Saxon times, when a manor stood here.

But its real history gets under way with Stephen Langton, a one-time resident. He was an Archbishop of Canterbury who was largely responsible for drawing up the Magna Carta and presenting it to King John.

Other notables followed the path from altar to Sussex quietness and Slindon House became the summer palace of the Archbishops of Canterbury.

The murdered primate St. Thomas of Canterbury walked the lawns here. So, too, did St. Richard, a bishop of Chichester and John Morton, Archbishop of Canterbury in the second half of the 15th century.

But to be a Catholic was not always as socially safe as spiritually uplifting. When Sir Garret Kempe rebuilt the house on the foundations of the old archbishops' building in Queen Elizabeth's day he had a secret chapel incorporated in the roof so Catholics could worship a few floors nearer their God and safe from religious persecution.

Stopham

Stopham Bridge, set in the lush countryside of the village with the same name near Pulborough, is justifiably the most beautiful in Sussex.

It was built to carry travellers from Petworth to Pulborough in 1309 and restored in the 16th century.

But it certainly wasn't built to carry cars and today they only cross it one way at a time. And there have been many that haven't made it even one way, either crashing into its stony walls or sometimes through them into the river.

The bridge is made up of six small arches and one high arch in the middle. Set into the 60 yards of roadway it carries are 17 small recesses specially made, so more leisurely travellers on foot can stop to admire views of trees and river banks.

History does of course cross the bridge into Stopham itself.

The church is of early Norman origin, although it has been modified down the years. It has heraldic glass in the 15th century east window and 17th century Dutch glass in a window on the north.

Slindon

Slindon lies in the green heart of West Sussex in what naturalists and country lovers generally acknowledge to be some of the finest territory in the county.

The heart of this small village is Slindon Park, a manor house rebuilt in the 16th century which has been altered at various years throughout its subsequent history and which was extensively restored in 1918.

The park — with its beeches and verdant woodlands, is included in some 3,500 acres stretching up to Bignor Hill and Stane Street which now are secured for the nation by the vigilant guardianship of the National Trust.

As for the village and the people fortunate enough to live in its small 17th century flint cottages, theirs is the pleasure of having a church with a late Norman nave and a 13th century chancel for their spiritual edification.

The tower dates from the 16th century and the church was restored in 1866 when the aisles and chancel arch were rebuilt.

As for the font, this dates from the 13th century and in the south aisle is a 16th century effigy thought to be of Anthony St. Leger, who died in 1539. Made in wood, it is believed to be the only one of its kind in Sussex.

In the church too is a memorial to Archbishop Stephen Langton, who died in 1228 at Slindon Park.

Slindon

The Elizabethan house called Dedisham Manor at Slindon is now occupied by a dairy farmer. The house has a long and troubled history.

Once the Tregoz family lived here. In the parish church, sheltered in a niche and hands folded across her stomach, is one such lady who joined their ranks, Katherine Blount.

She acquired the local name of Lady Dedisham and every Easter Sunday a posy of flowers has a habit of appearing in her hand.

Today it's a long narrow building, with eight bedrooms and additions made throughout the years. Once it was almost certainly one wing of a larger house.

After the war damage had been repaired a convalescent home for schoolchildren was run from here and was dedicated in 1948 by the then Bishop of Chichester.

There's a reputed secret passage too, leading supposedly under a river to a neighbouring house.

Small Dole

There have been all kinds of pay-offs during history for those who have helped others during times of crisis. For example there's the Golding barn at Small Dole, a tiny parish on the Shoreham-Horsham road just south of Henfield.

Legend has it that the barn is the only remaining part of a farm which flourished here once and which was given to a Mr. Goldyng by none other than Oliver Cromwell, grateful for the good services rendered to him during the Civil War. Good service continues at the barn, which has been turned into a restaurant by Mr. John Bell.

Yet another sort of service used to be observed hereabouts, at Beeding, which is in the same parish as Small Dole.

Where the church and vicarage now stand there was once a monastery whose abbot is reputed to have given the gift of land to some people who wished to settle there back in history.

The gift was called a small dole, which is how the hamlet came by its unusual name.

Sompting

Sompting church incorporates classic Rhineland architecture rising against the English countryside.

Its tower has rightly been called the greatest architectural curiosity in the country. It is the only example we have of a Rheinish helm roof — the sort that makes the Rhineland look such a far away and fairytale place on those travel posters.

The church itself is wholly Norman. It was rebuilt by the Knight Templars, to whom the Saxon church had been granted in 1154.

When the Templars were suppressed Sompting went to the Knights of St. John and they in turn added their contributions to the structure.

The tower itself is about 19sq. ft. in plan, and has no buttresses but is strengthened at the corners by pilasters of rectangular long and short stones.

The west doorway was altered in the 15th century and on the north of the tower is a moulded 14th century arch that originally opened into a chapel which has now fallen into ruins.

Inside the church is colourful and interesting. Many of the carved stones are believed to date back to the original Saxon church.

A later carving of a lady in a wimple is placed high on a window ledge and so is rather easy to miss.

But the Easter Sepulchre in the north wall of the chancel is the tomb of Richard Burre, who died in 1527.

Southease

If you think that history only started in 1066 do visit one of the finest churches in Sussex. It's at Southease and is the famous round-towered building with a charter dating all the way back to 966!

Before the time of William the Conqueror, the Anglo-Saxon King Edgar had made out the Southease charter to Hyde Abbey Winchester. The historic document — now in the British Museum — named "the church of Sueise with 28 hides of land and the church of Titelescumbe (Telscombe) with two hides . . ." to the abbey.

The strange name by which Southease was then called came from the Old English Sup-haes, meaning southern wood. Most of the church that remains today facing its beautiful green is Norman. Its round tower is one of only three such towers in Sussex, the other two being in the Ouse gap at Piddinghoe and Lewes.

The towers are reputed to have been built out of chalk flints because quarried stone was not readily available in the area. Some also say that they were built to serve as beacon towers at a time when the Ouse was navigable and Southease was a flourishing fishing village.

On the walls of the church nave is a notable series of 13th century paintings discovered by one Clive Rouse in 1935. Those on the north side depict scenes from the Life of Christ while those on the west show Christ in Majesty. They are thought to have been painted by monks.

In those far off days the church was a good deal larger and down the centuries has lost its original chancel and two aisles.

Southwick

To the coast road tripper from the industrial Midlands, Southwick and neighbouring towns must seem like a home from grimy home. The wharves which connect it with Portslade, the science-fiction-like industrial complexes shining out at night over Shoreham Harbour, all make the area at first glance something like the antithesis of the travel brochure's verdant image of a green and lush Sussex.

First glances can be deceiving, step behind the coast road, with its never ceasing traffic, and there opens before you Southwick Green, an oasis of quiet charm that goes back to the days before the industrial age.

The history of Southwick is well charted all the way back to the Romans. Near Southdown Road and just to the east of the Green are the remains of a large Roman villa of the traditional courtyard type and which the experts tell us was occupied in the second to fourth centuries. The villa has been excavated by the Sussex Archaeological Trust and is still under their care.

Steyning

Once Steyning was a good deal nearer the ocean than it is today and up until the end of the 14th century boasted a flourishing harbour. But then silt saw the end of that role.

Time and the shift towards larger political units also robbed the town of its Parliamentary status when in 1832 it was disenfranchised and lost the two MPs it had sent to Whitehall since the days of Edward I.

History relates that St. Cuthman founded and built a timber church with his own hands, where Ethelwulf, king of Essex and father of King Alfred, was buried in 858.

That was the beginning of a town that in its day went on to be one of the largest in the country. Edward the Confessor granted his estates there to the Benedictine abbey of Fecamp in Normandy and the 12th century saw the establishment of a collegiate church.

On the suppression of alien and foreign priories in 1415 it passed to the Crown but soon after was conferred on Syon Abbey in Middlesex by Edward IV.

Today the building is one of the loveliest churches in Sussex. The surviving part of the cruciform church built around 1150 by the Fecamp monks is the nave with the aisles and crossings.

But much of the rest of the building has had to be rebuilt after the church had virtually slid into a state of collapse by the end of the 16th century.

Steyning

A property steeped in history in the High Street at Steyning is Chanctonbury Cottage, once called Brittons. A 1542 account by a minister of Henry VIII mentions the house by name and says there was due a quit rent of "14 pence from Thoms. Adams per annum for one burgage called Bryten lately Arnolds."

A quit rent was money paid for a house in lieu of service rent paid to the lord of the manor, a sort of medieval ground rent in fact.

The thatched roof cottage figures in Steyning's past again. The old court book of the town mentions the property four times — plus its quit rent.

It stated: "In 1699 Mary Walder, a widow, held freely of this borough for a yearly rent of 14p a messuage, barn and a croft called Brittons."

She died in that year. John Turner, her heir, came next followed by one John Mordaunt in 1732 and Sir John Honeywood, the MP for Steyning, in 1784.

Nearer the present day the cottage was sold by the Wiston estate in 1940 and has stayed in private occupancy ever since.

Its wooden tiles must have echoed with the passing of many a tread, including that of poet W. B. Yeats, who penned some of his most famous poems when he lived in the area during the mid-war years.

Storrington

Parham House, near Storrington, was built in 1577. Only four ownerships have spanned the manor in 1,000 years. St. Dunstan bought it in about 950 and gave it to the Abbey of Westminster. Robert Palmer came by the manor for £1,258 in 1540. In 1601 the newly-built house was bought by one Thomas Bysshop, a Henfield barrister. And in 1922 Parham was sold to the Hon. Clive Pearson, whose family still own it.

The Great Hall is your entrance to the Elizabethan world. At one end is the original carved oak screen set into the wall, and round other walls is fine Elizabethan panelling. Look out for two small windows set high above the screen. Recently discovered behind plaster, they allowed stewards to look down into the hall to keep an eye on servants. Also recently discovered — the original fireplace.

For a vivid contrast in footwear, take a look at the colossal Cromwellian boots.

More fascinating still, the colossal narwhal tusks, complete with case. Elizabethan explorers brought them back from their travels and people believed they were tusks from the unicorn.

In the Great Parlor are mostly royal portraits. Here, too, is a painting by Van Dyck of Ann Kirke, supposed to be one of his best of an Englishwoman. There are delicately worked Venetian wall mirrors, and among outstanding examples of needlework is a set of six French high-backed walnut chairs with elaborate needlework, dating from about 1690.

Thakeham

In the Domesday Book it was mentioned as Taceham. That meant thatched homestead. There's not much thatch left now. And time has changed the name to Thakeham. But one thing is certain — the village today is as much of a rural picture as it was then.

Thakeham lies inland from Worthing and near the village of Ashington in the lush and gently rolling countryside of West Sussex.

Its character has come down the centuries with the environmental protection that is earned by remaining a small community.

The church is a building of splendidly large proportions. King Henry II was on the throne when its stout timbers were settled into place, and the Normans had been in the country for only 84 years.

The builders used largely sandstone and ironstone and pews with carved leaves and Tudor roses were introduced about 1500.

But more than that the church boasts 16th century brasses and altar-tombs and one in particular which is the only specimen of its kind in Sussex.

It is one William Apsley, who died in 1527 and it bears his effigy in armour incised in an alabaster slab.

Standing near the church is the 16th century Church House, under its sturdy roof of Horsham slabs. It was originally two cottages but they have been converted into a timber-framed house of great beauty, and it is almost certain that at one time a priest's house occupied the site.

Trotton

It's perhaps an over fond fancy to think the ecological-environmental awakening could start country water mills turning again. But what an indirect benefit if an energy crisis gave us back Terwick Mill at Trotton for example.

Now the mill languishes in both senses in superb country near Midhurst. Today, it is converted into dwellings, a silent reminder of a bygone industry.

It was in 1966 that the brothers Ayling sadly brought the machinery to a stop, ending a family spell at the mill that went back through their father and his father too.

In its day Terwick Mill was big with its own storemen, administrative staff and carters and clerical staff too. But concentration of milling at giant centres had thrown the Ayling brothers back on pig and poultry food as a last resort before that too proved uneconomical and was overtaken by time.

There were two parts to the "modern" mill at the end of its career. The larger and more recent was dated at 1746 and the older part was thought to be at least 100 years older than that. Walls were two feet thick in the original section.

Terwick was, in fact, two mills in one. It had two separate water wheels of different sizes side by side, a feature still retained today.

And in its prime that helped win it a reputation for the finest ground Sussex oats. From the lower floor sacks of grain were hoisted through three storeys to the mill top by chain and via a series of trap doors.

Terwick Mill was thought to have been the last fully operational water mill in Sussex, but was without electricity right to the end. Midnight rush grinding had to be carried with emergency help from oil lamps.

But electricity wasn't the prime need, with the Rother providing all the power wanted without a puff of grimy smoke or a smut of industrial pollution on the green countryside.

Warnham

Shelley was born at Warnham, on the borders of Sussex and Surrey, and as a child he lived behind the imposing walls of Field Place.

The parish church of the small village figured large in the family's life, except for Shelley himself.

His baptism on September 7, 1792, is recorded in the register—spelt wrongly by the incumbent who wrote Bysshe with only one 's' and had to add the other later.

The little chapel now used as a vestry was provided by the Shelley family in the 16th century and in 1771 his father, Sir Timothy Shelley, presented the church plate.

Generations of the Shelleys are buried in the church, including the poet's two sisters. But what the Shelley family thought of the marital and rebellious excesses of their poetic progeny is perhaps best indicated by the memorial tablet there to Shelley's son Charles, who died aged 11.

It doesn't mention Shelley at all but instead refers to Charles as being just the grandson of Sir Timothy.

Shelley isn't the only person who has helped to make this quiet Sussex village famous. Sir Henry Harben helped put it on a map other than that of romantic poetry.

He founded the Prudential Assurance Company. His descendants for many years lived in the family home at Warnham Lodge and in 1891 he presented the village with the customary village hall.

The church itself is over 700 years old and was extensively restored in 1885.

Its colourful history is given added dimensions by an old map which indicated that it began as a shrine in the Wealden Forest and stood at the crossroads of two long forgotten tracks.

West Burton

It's almost a sin to write about a lost hamlet like West Burton. They now run the risk of foraging trippers actually finding it!

But there is a safety factor built in — there isn't much of it . . . not enough to even promote up to the status of a village.

West Burton, near Bury — but a long way in reality from anywhere — is just a mere quadrilateral of lanes and houses. And Cooke's House is a fine example of what one can see.

It was once Coke's House, the owner will explain, but the subsequent mispronunciation made her change it back to the original.

The earliest known date for the house is 1588 when it was called Hall's Place, after the family who lived in the property. But the building is older than that and nearby Roman occupation of Bignor makes for a possibility that it could date back as a housing site to those times.

Later the Cookes bought the house and occupied it for centuries. But those earlier residents left more than a name. Sir Richard Hall went from here for a new life in the land of America in 1643. He prospered and England dropped over the horizon of his family's lives. Yet not in their memories.

American voices coming up the front path recently heralded latter day transatlantic Halls doing the time-honoured thing of checking up on their ancestors — the West Burton ones in this case.

They must have found the house pretty much as Sir Richard had left it, sturdy under its Horsham slab roof and West Burton stone walls — a textbook example of a small manor house, missing only a small chapel knocked down in the grounds last century.

Westdean

Westdean and Irish-woman Lady Rhoda Birley are what you might call mutually complementary forces.

The one provides the greenery and rural charm of a picturesque and beautiful Sussex village hidden away in the Downs near Cuckmere Valley, just along the coast from Seaford.

The other proves all the sparkle, wit and artistic interests that have put Westdean on more than just the geographical map.

Backcloth to it all is the superb house of Charleston Manor. It was the home until his death of portrait painter Sir Oswald Birley, now buried in Westdean churchyard.

Nowhere could have provided him with greater inspiration than the manor. The hamlet of Westdean itself is said to have been the centre of Southern England's fight against marauding Danes.

Another historic legend states that, around 850, King Alfred came here to build a palace, and topped it by also building a shipyard — the sea then came this far up the valley.

Admittedly, there's more conjecture and imagination than proof about all this, and the origins of Charleston Manor are not certain either.

Lady Birley says the older parts were built for William the Conqueror's cup-bearer around 1080 and claims the manor is one of the oldest occupied houses in the country.

Certainly parts of the manor have definitely been dated to around 1200. This oldest section is the south wing, which has a hall on the upper floor.

But it's the great Tithe Barn that the public knows best. It's here that Lady Birley's artistic dreams found their opening in the annual festivals for music, art and horticulture.

Lady Birley believes the barn was built in the 15th or 16th centuries. Her husband turned it into a studio and theatre before the Second World War but it fell into disrepair after his death.

Fell is the operative word because it nearly did. But Lady Birley's inspiration saved it at the 11th hour and she had the building restored over an 18-month period with the assistance of small Government and county council grants — and a lot of help from her friends.

The thatch was replaced by tiles and the 200ft. towering building entered a new life with its role as a country culture centre.

Westham

Brian Duppa was vicar of the parish of Westham, near Pevensey, from 1625 until 1638 and later went on to be a chancellor of Oxford and in turn Bishop of Chichester, Salisbury and Winchester.

Perhaps it's the Westham air that is stimulating. And then again perhaps the historic splendour of the church more than normally inspires those who both preach and worship there.

This large building is partly Norman and partly of the 14th and 15th centuries. Those with an eye for church archaeology will be able to detect a few remains of the Norman cruciform church dating back to about 1080.

The fine nave arcade and wide north aisle were built in the 14th century, when the fine tower was also added to replace a central one from an earlier date.

The 15th century saw the re-building of the chancel and the adding of a fine porch of flint and stone chequer. The beautiful carved oak rood-screen and the massive beam of the same period have been restored and replaced in their old position under the chancel arch.

Winchelsea

It seems almost an irony of history to refer to "New Winchelsea." This coastal village of East Sussex has a maritime past that makes it one of the most important and colourful tourist spots in the county.

But the newness is relative. It was in 1292 that King Edward I founded a New Winchelsea on a virgin site after a great storm in 1287 changed the course of the River Rother, guaranteeing a new prosperity for nearby Rye and destroying finally Old Winchelsea.

The new town as it was in those days was laid out in 800 plots and tenants paid an annual rent to the Crown.

Winchelsea began to flourish again, becoming an outlet for the Sussex wool trade and becoming incorporated in 1298.

But it didn't always attract the right sort of attention. During the 14th and 15th centuries marauding Frenchmen from across the Channel made repeated attacks along the Sussex coast.

The years 1339 and 1360 are recorded in Winchelsea as being ones of virtual seaborne invasion. Although it beat off the attack during which Rye was burned in 1377 the town was finally sacked in 1380 and abandoned by its townfolk for some time.

It was doubtless with its vulnerability from the sea in mind that one of Winchelsea's most picturesque houses was built in the 14th century and which later became known as The Armoury.

Winchelsea

The parish church of Winchelsea is the crowning glory of one of the most beautiful villages in the county.

The church was begun soon after the foundation of Winchelsea itself. It started as the Church of St. Thomas of Canterbury, but was rededicated by Henry VIII to St. Thomas the Apostle because of his hate for the religious rebel that Becket had been.

The original concept for the church was on a grand scale and if it had been finished to plan it would have been one of the largest in Sussex. But it never was, possibly because of the repeated French raids along this stretch of the South Coast or perhaps more simply because during its building Winchelsea ceased to become quite such an important settlement.

Today the building is made up of the chancel, with its north and south chapels. Gone is the tower and it's possible that the nave was never even started before the builders lost their enthusiasm.

But what was unfinished is forgotten by comparison with the grace and splendour of the church as it is today. Inside is a wealth of medieval monuments and one of the county's finest collections of recumbent effigies, with their elaborate canopies.

The most lasting impression is the stained glass. Although much of it is in the modern Kentish pattern style, its gentle blues and reds fill the church with colour.

In the chapel of St. Nicholas are the early 14th century tombs of the Alard family — who later became known as the first admirals of England. In their day they were a powerful South Coast family, by virtue of being both shipowners and wine merchants.

Withyham

In actual buildings, the hamlet of Withyham — up on the borders of Sussex near East Grinstead — consists of little more than a church, a few cottages and the charming Dorset Arms Inn.

But historically it is rich in associations with the past. The old timbers and Georgian staircase of the inn have echoed to the tread of customers since the 16th century.

And the church contains the family chapel of the Sackville family, earls of Dorset. It was originally a 14th century building but it was struck by lightning and seriously damaged in 1663 and all that remains are the tower, the north wall of the nave and the south wall. The rest dates from the 1672 restoration and rebuilding in the 19th century.

The Sackvilles, who have had their seat at nearby Buckhurst House since approximately 1200, have their tomb in the vault beneath the north chapel of the church.

In the centre of the chapel is the table-tomb of Thomas Sackville, the young son of the fifth Earl of Dorset. It was fashioned in 1678 by Danish sculptor Caius Gabriel Cibber and is an acknowledged masterpiece.

On the walls are many monuments to the Sackville family, including one to the third duke, who died in 1799. He was a noted cricketer and helped make the rules of the M.C.C.

In the east window is a stained glass which traces the descent of the Sackvilles from Herbrand de Sauqueville, who is thought to have come to England with William the Conqueror's invading army.

Worthing

It was the Saxons who first extensively settled in Worthing. Long before this major coastal resort of West Sussex gained a reputation for summer sunshine and as a premier retirement haven, these early farming settlers forsook the Downs to move instead to the fertile coastal plain that still has a market gardening industry of importance.

Saxon occupation in the area still lives on through the number of places with names ending in "ing". a Saxon phrase meaning "the people of."

But the Romans and pre-historic man left their traces in what has become the modern town and on the Downs northwards of present urban development.

Yet for many years Worthing was a small manor attached to the more important parish it was eventually to swallow up.

Worthing was first put on the map in 1798 when George III sent his youngest daughter, Princess Amelia, to this particular spot on the South Coast for her health.

Later the Prince Regent and his daughter Princess Charlotte came too and by the 19th century their example had been taken up by thousands of others seeking Worthing's fresh air and bracing climate.

History goes further back at West Tarring, once an outlying village but now part of Worthing borough. The manor was given by King Athelstan in 941 to the Archbishop of Canterbury.

The remains of an archiepiscopal palace remain at the corner of the High Street and consist of a 14th-15th century hall and the undercroft of a solar of pre-1250.

In nearby Church Road is a famous fig garden planted mostly in 1745. But some of the trees are thought to be even older and one is traditionally supposed to have been planted by Archbishop Thomas a Becket when he visited the palace.

The mother church of Worthing is still to be found at Broadwater. It is an interesting cruciform building with a late Norman tower and mostly dating from the 13th century. Here is the tomb of Thomas West, the eighth Lord de la Warr, who was a leading supporter of Henry VII and who died in 1525.